MODERNITY AND PROGRESS

MODERNITY AND PROGRESS
Fitzgerald, Hemingway, Orwell

RONALD BERMAN

THE UNIVERSITY OF ALABAMA PRESS
Tuscaloosa

Typeface: AGaramond

∞

The paper on which this book is printed meets the minimum requirements of American
National Standard for Information Science—Permanence of Paper for Printed Library
Materials, ANSI Z39.48-1984.

Library of Congress Cataloging-in-Publication Data

Berman, Ronald.
Modernity and progress : Fitzgerald, Hemingway, Orwell / Ronald Berman.
p. cm.
Includes bibliographical references and index.
ISBN 978-0-8173-5430-5
1. American fiction—20th century—History and criticism. 2. Modernism (Literature)—
English-speaking countries. 3. Fitzgerald, F. Scott (Francis Scott), 1896–1940—Criticism and
interpretation. 4. Hemingway, Ernest, 1899–1961—Criticism and interpretation. 5. Orwell,
George, 1903–1950—Criticism and interpretation. 6. Literature and history—English-
speaking countries. 7. Progress in literature. I. Title.
PS374.M535B475 2005
813'.5209—dc22
2004029703

Chapter 1 first appeared in *The F. Scott Fitzgerald Review* 1 (2002). Chapter 3 first appeared in
The F. Scott Fitzgerald Review 2 (2003). Chapter 5 is reprinted from *The Hemingway Review* 23,
no. 2 (Spring 2004). Chapter 6 first appeared in *The St. John's Review,* Spring 1984.

For

Barbara and Kathy, Andrew, Linda and Matt, Julie, Mick,
Joshua and Sam, Bern and Dorothy

Contents

MODERNITY AND PROGRESS

Introduction

Nearly every significant detail of Fitzgerald's authorial life is linked to a date. He locates us in the period 1919–29 as no other writer does, making the sharpest of distinctions between things happening, say, in 1919, 1922, and 1927. The values of realism are so well served that he is invoked as evidence by historians. But the passage of time matters as much as accurate location within it. In Fitzgerald, as in the decade of the twenties, change or continuance in time is a measure of progress.

Chronology is a conscious part of Fitzgerald's narratives, with his characters making it part of their self-conception. Here is one of his timetables for success in "Winter Dreams" of 1922:

> "Let's start right," she interrupted herself suddenly. "Who are you, anyhow?"
>
> For a moment Dexter hesitated. Then:
>
> "I'm nobody," he announced. "My career is largely a matter of futures."[1]

The passage proceeds in the language of beginning, halting, continuing, and culminating, but the idea of *becoming* is most compelling. Fitzgerald's language follows a national script about personal change through success, a script his characters know. Before amusing us, Dexter Green and Judy

Jones amuse each other in a *paso doble* around the linked quantities of time and identity. Their phrasing is allusive in more than one way. We have for a long time understood that there is a kind of greatness in the assumption of a self. Novels from *David Copperfield* through *Kim* to *The Portrait of the Artist as a Young Man* would not be intelligible without a central act of self-creation. At this point in our history, "futures" refers to commodities more than it does to philosophies. The term is oppositional, and the passage evokes large meanings that have become compressed into little, material forms.

In 1920, shortly before this story appeared, George Santayana's *Character and Opinion in the United States* had suggested that Americans each had their own "personal philosophy" based on empirical truth. Such belief "regards only the future" and has little use for the past. What was vulnerable to it? The "materialism of youth." Who were most likely to believe themselves "*verified*" by materialism? "The younger cosmopolitan America."[2] Fitzgerald stated in an interview of 1922—it seems refractive—that "the philosophy of ever so many young people to-day" was all empiricism with no "tradition" to guide it.[3] Something odd had happened to the idea of personal progress. It had become movement without destination.

In another narrative of 1922, on his way to his office George Babbitt drives by the hill on which his neighborhood, Floral Heights, has spread itself out. He is deeply pleased by the absence of nature. Its accidental beauty can't compete with "immaculate" lawns flashing by and the "amazing comfort" of the homes they enclose. Babbitt has begun his meditation by thinking of time's progress and then of his own, from twenty years before when there was only useless wilderness here to the precise grid of streets replacing it.[4] A Fitzgerald story of 1922 depicts the same order of experience in a different way. Over a period of thirty years, country fields in the South have changed into city streets. Advancing geometrical lines of houses represent the importation of northern style—and also the current national principle of moving either "up" or "on."[5] In this case, does alteration of the past guarantee progress? By 1929, *Middletown* (in the chapter "Why Do They Work So Hard?") will cite a factory interview: "They're just working. They don't know what for. They're just in a rut and keep on in it, doing the same monotonous work every day, and wondering when a slump will come and they will be laid off."[6] That suggests why Dalyrimple goes wrong and why George Wilson—inert in a moving world—is so allegorical a figure in *The Great Gatsby.*

Babbitt's faith in progress has an honorable ancestry. Mark Twain wrote to Walt Whitman in 1889: "Wait thirty years and then look over the earth! . . . Man almost at his full stature at last!"[7] As stated by Herbert Spencer, who was the great original of this school of thought, progress was inevitable not only for organic life but in "the evolution of Society."[8] In a more modulated way, Bertrand Russell later defined his own generational expectations: "There was to be ordered progress throughout the world, no revolutions, a gradual cessation of war, and an extension of parliamentary government to all those unfortunate regions which did not yet enjoy it."[9] The rubrics of progressivism until the twenties were "Transforming America" and "Ending Class Conflict."[10] But there was bound to be conflict between formless reality and imagined order. Looking backward, Russell added this to his recollections: "The hopes of that period seem now a little absurd."[11]

Walter Lippmann summed up the predicament of embodying ideals:

Evolution first in Darwin himself, and then more elaborately in Herbert Spencer, was a "progress towards perfection." The stereotype represented by such words as "progress" and "perfection" was composed fundamentally of mechanical inventions. . . . the country village will become the great metropolis, the modest building a skyscraper, what is small shall be big, what is slow shall be fast, what is poor shall be rich, what is few shall be many; whatever is shall be more so. . . . The ideal confuses excellence with size, happiness with speed, and human nature with contraption. . . . With the stereotype of "progress" before their eyes, Americans have in the mass seen little that did not accord with that progress. They saw the expansion of cities, but not the accretion of slums; they cheered the growth statistics, but refused to consider overcrowding; they pointed with pride to their growth, but would not see the drift . . .[12]

Fitzgerald was to invoke one important aspect of "drift" in *The Great Gatsby.*[13] And he worked out a dialectic of time and progress in a number of stories that take place below the Mason-Dixon Line. Lionel Trilling's essay on *The Bostonians* explains why the South might be important as an opposing element in fiction:

The two principles are constant, although circumstances change their particular manifestations and the relative values which they are to be judged to have. They may be thought of as energy and inertia; or spirit and matter; or spirit and letter; or force and form; or creation and possession; or Libido and Thanatos. In their simpler manifestations the first term of the grandiose duality is generally regarded with unqualified sympathy and is identified with the ideality of youth, or with truth, or with art, or with America. . . . for North and South, as James understands them, represent the two opposing elements in that elaborate politics of culture which, all over the civilized world, has been the great essential subject of the literature of the nineteenth and twentieth centuries.[14]

Fitzgerald considered himself heir to the nineteenth-century tradition and came naturally to its polarities of energy and inertia, spirit and matter, stasis and change. In *The Great Gatsby* Daisy Fay and Jordan Baker have been shaped by the passage from Louisville to New York. That is part of becoming "sophisticated," meaning, living with contradictory moral views about reality. A number of characters in Fitzgerald make (or decline) the transformation from the provinces to Metropolis, from the past to the present: "Carmen from the South," otherwise known as Sally Carrol Happer in "The Ice Palace"; Jim Powell in "The Jelly-Bean" and "Dice, Brassknuckles & Guitar"; and Ailie Calhoun in "The Last of the Belles." On another but still serious level are Littleboy Le Moyne in "Basil and Cleopatra," who replays the Civil War twice in one day, and that "Southern girl" in "The Ice Palace" who "came up" north and had to leave for telling the truth.[15] These characters are self-consciously involved in the cultural wars of the early part of the twentieth century. We understand that Fitzgerald's South is defined by the North, with which it has a dialectical relationship. The North is where human "energy" and "vitality," those great honorifics of William James, can be deployed in the pursuit of a new self. But, as Fitzgerald's own phrase goes, the price was high. His figures become involved in "the enormous flux of American life" and must choose between the kinds of polarities listed by Trilling.[16] Balzac ends *Old Goriot* with a challenge to Paris by Rastignac, but one of Fitzgerald's characteristic endings is the surrender to and exile from modern times.

Hemingway was at one point interested in viewing character native to "the Southern part of the United States."[17] But his view of America—one might say his quarrel with America—took the form of opposed styles and intellectual habits. The evaluation of American "civilization" was one of the great themes of magazine culture, and there was much for Hemingway to read about the making of Americans. He was himself read by those who wanted to understand that subject. Walter Lippmann wrote in 1929: "if one turns to the smarter of those novelists who describe the doings of the more advanced set of those who are experimenting with life—to, for example, Mr. Aldous Huxley or Mr. Ernest Hemingway,—one will discover in their tragic farces the picture of a society which is at bottom in despair because, though it is more completely absorbed in the pursuit of love than in anything else, it has lost the sense of any ultimate importance inherent in the experience."[18] Lippmann added that Hemingway in particular was a reliable judge of a "generally devalued world."[19] He means that Hemingway is both perceptive and morally obtuse.

In 1939, against the moralistic grain, Lionel Trilling argued that Hemingway was to be valued precisely *because of* his "negation." He had in the twenties shown life as it was, tragic, unlikely to be changed by political ideology. That had alarmed into reflection those "progressive professional and middle-class forces" who wanted literature to support good causes. When progress became entwined with political ideology, the culture of midcult liberalism demanded novels with opinions.[20] It wanted a literature committed to social justice. And in the next generation, Dwight Macdonald identified some cumulative effects of "progress" on style:

A tepid ooze of Midcult is spreading everywhere. Psychoanalysis is expounded sympathetically and superficially in popular magazines. . . . movies aren't as terrible as they once were, but they aren't so good either; the general level of taste and craftsmanship has risen but there are no more great exceptions like Griffith, von Stroheim, Chaplin, Keaton; Orson Welles was the last. . . . The question, of course, is whether all this is merely growing pains. . . . The danger is that the values of Midcult, instead of being transitional—"the price of progress"—may now themselves become a debased, permanent standard.

I see no reason Midcult may not be stabilized as the norm in our culture.[21]

Images argue: one notes how few straight lines there are in Hemingway and how many margins into which they disappear. His terrain in all its indistinctness and circularity derives from Twain, Conrad, and Cézanne, with whom it has metaphysical affinities. The idea of progress is a straight-line set of ideas—Isaiah Berlin sees it in fact as a "path" temporarily blocked by "unreason."[22] Straight lines imply "universality, objectivity, immutability . . . rational organisation."[23] They entitle themselves, although not in Hemingway, to arrive at clearly understood destinations. In Hemingway, a railroad track vanishes into marsh, a trail into a lake, a hunting path into the brush. More than one kind of demarcation takes place when leaving the straight for the indeterminate. Francis Macomber, for example, understands what it is to leave the road for the savannah.

Hemingway wrote a number of stories about the American mind, comparing our culture to that of Europe. These stories, like his novels of the twenties, explore the failures of intellectual style. In one of his neglected works, "Banal Story," Hemingway examined the unreal world of rational certainty. His vehicle was the *Forum,* a magazine dedicated to progress in its myriad forms. One might within three or four reading-minutes be assured that war would be abolished or the cure to all diseases found—or that life could be made rational and literary style perfected. Hemingway played the role of a reader, going over a number of fake ideas, using them to illustrate his own resistance to perfectibility. Needless to insist, he did a memorable job of deconstruction.[24] But if that constituted his whole resistance to "progress," and if the same could be said of Fitzgerald, then they would have been satirists on a moderate scale, so moderate as not to have been serious rivals to, say, Sinclair Lewis. In what ways did they advance thought? There are two essential parts of the equation with which I began, not only "progress" but "time." The former seems more promising because of its vulnerability to the comparison of ideal to fact. But it was the latter that turned out to have heavier caliber as a subject of modernism.

～

Fitzgerald and Hemingway wrote in a world in which the concept of linear time was breaking down. Gertrude Stein described a continuous present; Bertrand Russell wrote that images of the past were retained within and affected a given moment of perception; Walter Lippmann identified social time, immediate time, and perceptual time, all of which differed and could be illusory. Above all was the concept of relative time stated by Einstein in 1905. It echoed in the lives of Fitzgerald and Hemingway because Einstein received his Nobel Prize in 1921, a year important for the development of both writers. Fitzgerald maneuvered between meanings, and it is, I think, a mistake to read his hundreds of invocations of time as if they were signposts of realism. His characters begin with confidence measured by time, but they discover lapses in sequence. The theme resonates because the great oppositions in Fitzgerald are not only between wealth and middle-class aspiration; they are between different degrees of metaphysical confidence in the way things are. One of the ways in which this conflict is stated is by reference to the changing meanings of time.

In 1928, Bertrand Russell considered relationships fundamental to perception and, necessarily, to the account of perception in fiction. His subjects are those of the novel, that is, the location of mind in time and space:

> Take the notion of "progress": if the time-order is arbitrary, there will be progress or retrogression according to the convention adopted in measuring time. The notion of distance in space is of course also affected: two observers . . . will arrive at different estimates of the distance between two places, if the observers are in rapid relative motion. It is obvious that the very idea of distance has become vague, because distance must be between material things, not points of empty space (which are fictions); and it must be the distance at a given time, because the distance between any two bodies is continually changing; and a given time is a subjective notion.[25]

Russell's purpose is not only to elucidate Einstein but to point out that all certainties that derive from ideas of substance within time must now change; that is to say, without being paradoxical, all relationships are relative. As a recent cultural history puts it, by the twenties the breakdown of ideas about time and space necessarily changed ideas about all other human categories. There were no longer very many "fixed boundaries and beliefs."[26]

Few subjects interested Hemingway more than the connection of act and belief. He made a long series of references in his novels and stories to the limitations of thinking without the validation of experience. Without a context, his remarks will inevitably seem anti-intellectual. But they have a close connection to the leading philosophy of the twenties. If Lippmann echoes Hemingway on opinion, Hemingway echoes Bertrand Russell and Wittgenstein on the nature of thought. There was in the twenties an extraordinary burst of intellectual activity about the way thought proceeded, its connection to either senses or conceptions, and the overwhelming problem of the language of statement. Bertrand Russell had in 1921 concluded that mind and body were of course connected, but not indisputably, through the mechanism of thought. He was much interested in the ways that all mammals reacted to "a certain sensory situation" and was quite willing to demythologize "any need of thought" for "habitual action."[27] This must have been grist to the mill for a writer so intensely interested in hunting and the corrida. In fact, Russell anticipated Hemingway's own conclusions. And, of course, so did Wittgenstein during the twenties. Later, *Philosophical Investigations* (on the subject of "what is *thinking?*") became central to modern ideas about the relationship of act to thought and thought to language.[28] Wittgenstein's interest—notably utilitarian—did not focus on the supposedly ennobling aspect of thought. He simply wanted to see how observation became statement.

Hemingway makes detailed references to the expression of thought. In one unexpected place, "The Undefeated," we begin by reading that Maera tries but cannot "realize the thought" that language fails to express. Then we read that instincts and words have little equivalence, that experiential knowledge is superior to abstract knowledge, that action is by no means dependent on thought—in fact, it may best proceed "without thought." Finally, we realize that to be "conscious" of the moment is not to be restricted to thought interpreting it.[29] "The Killers" is famously about the disjunction between thought and fact, and has literally dozens of passages involving the use of "idea," "think," and "know." Nothing designated means what we "think" it does, except for "bright boys" who mistake the inherently tenuous connection of fact to idea.[30]

The vocabulary of "thinking" is extensive in Hemingway, as is the opposition between empirical discovery and reliance on intellectual illusion. Hemingway's "Soldier's Home," "Now I Lay Me," and especially *Death in the Afternoon* restate the intricate problem. Here it is seen in compressed form in a dialogue between the priest and Frederic Henry from *A Farewell to Arms:* "I never think and yet when I begin to talk I say the things I have found out in my mind without thinking."[31] That kind of critique did not mean that Hemingway rejected thought—the issue was never instinct versus intelligence. He believed, instead, that thought needed to be arrived at empirically, resisted when it became dogma, tested by experience.

Old connections did not hold, but new ones were available: "Cézanne broke up space by offering more than one point of view on a single canvas and by dragging the background into the foreground of a landscape. Then, in the 1900s, Pablo Picasso, Georges Braque, and other Cubist painters rejected the conventional representation of homogeneous, three-dimensional space. Cubist painting offered many spaces, many perspectives; it even exposed the interior of objects."[32] In fact, Paul Cézanne accomplished significantly more than changing perspective, and Hemingway repeatedly called his work to mind. In no case was he more specific than in stating his debt to Cézanne. He often acknowledged that he tried to write the way that Cézanne painted. It should be noted that he was thinking of landscapes and that Cézanne's landscapes came into new prominence in the twenties. The appearance in 1927 of Roger Fry's *Cézanne: A Study of His Development* brought together overwhelming arguments about the painter's ideas, technique, and place in the history of painting. Art historians still use this book, which has been called the most influential ever done on its subject. After Fry, it was understood that Cézanne had in some important ways structured the perceptions of modernism. His became the dominant idea of style and of engagement. Adding impetus to the argument was the appearance of Virginia Woolf's life of Fry in 1940. Woolf argued that *both* Cézanne and Fry were culture-heroes engaged in the creation of an artistic identity contravening received opinion. In fact, both exemplified the idea of first creating a technique and then personifying individualism against "the herd" of literate minds.[33] That should be kept in mind when thinking of the Lillian Ross interview of Hemingway at the Metropolitan Museum of Art. It was part of the context that Ross did not have the equipment to introduce.

I have studied the relationship of Hemingway and Cézanne from the point of view of art history. There is much material on the landscapes—they themselves have been newly cataloged—and there are original letters and interviews to sort through. Scholars have paid a great deal of attention to the alternate versions of those landscapes. Cézanne did many versions of *Mont Sainte-Victoire* and was forthright in stating why. Many Cézanne paintings contain the motifs of *la route tournante*. Certain of his landscapes like *Le Mont Sainte-Victoire au-dessus de la Route du Tholenet* are repetitive. The large group of paintings that contain the signature motif of the bend in the road (a major Cézanne painting even has that title) seems to have been especially important to Hemingway. It is a complex subject that I have tried to outline in these ways: first, both Hemingway and Cézanne use the road motif recurrently. That can be seen in a number of the stories and especially in *The Sun Also Rises*. Second, the use of this kind of pictorial geometry is not confined to dividing visual planes: it is invariably directed against a part of the canvas that is inaccessible. One of the most important statements that Cézanne made about his landscapes is that not everything in them is explicable. He argued that it might be better to leave a blank space in a canvas than to depict something he did not understand, and he actually did this in certain paintings.[34] Hemingway relied on the post-Impressionist technique of repetition in the depiction of landscape, a technique designed by Cézanne to capture perception—insofar as that might be possible—over time.

We can't study the fate of progress over time and the devolution of ideas without including Orwell. The centenary of his birth has made it necessary for us to think about him more closely if only because of the flood of reviews, opinions, and reassessments that have come over the dam. Most of these are devoted to his life and politics, which is not a bad thing. But they interpret his fiction, particularly *Nineteen Eighty-Four, as if it were explained by his life and politics.* The work now appearing on Orwell has been impregnated with biographical and intentional fallacies. Editorial critics have for a long time been reading Orwell as if he were a liberal Democrat or a conservative Republican. But no one knows how a novel might vote. Orwell wrote *Nineteen Eighty-Four* as a continuation of an ancient debate on how men and women should live. That is why O'Brien, one of its central figures, cannot stop appealing to history and, even more importantly, to its design. However, he invokes more than political history. One of the great texts on Orwell's mind and also on O'Brien's was transparently the *Politics* of Aristotle; a second was, I think, Freud's *Civilization and Its Discontents*. Aristotle provided Orwell with theory, example, even the language of description. The *Politics* is by no means restricted to making and enforcing laws; it concerns the way in which men and women live under different regimes. One of its most important arguments is that the policies of tyranny act "against everything likely to produce the two qualities of mutual confidence and a high spirit."[35] The ultimate aim of the despotic state is to break the "spirit" of its citizens and to prevent ordinary human association. Finally, Aristotle writes that the aim of despotism is "to sow mutual distrust and to foster discord between friend and friend."[36] There are statements on human association—especially the idea of betrayal—that Orwell has done nothing less than translate.

We expect the presence of Freud in any twentieth-century story of love and sexuality. Some particular Freudian arguments are put to work by Orwell, among them that myth—especially about the beginning and the end of things—is strongly rooted in the mind. *Civilization and Its Discontents,* which had appeared in the generation before *Nineteen Eighty-Four,* opened up new perspectives on ultimate social destiny. It became a guide to ideas about development through family, community, and state. One consequence was that it assumed political authority that it still retains. On the issue of what constitutes civilization, Orwell seems to have understood Freud. He used him to modernize much older ideas about human association. In fact, Freud himself depended on a version of the Idea of Progress that anticipated the plot of *Nineteen Eighty-Four:*

The last, but certainly not the least important, of the characteristic features of civilization remains to be assessed: the manner in which the relationships of men to one another, their social relationships, are regulated—relationships which affect a person as a neighbour, as a source of help, as another person's sexual object, as a member of a family and of a State. . . . The first requisite of civilization, therefore, is that of justice—that is, the assurance that a law once made will not be broken in favour of an individual. . . . The further course of cultural development seems to tend towards making the law no longer an expression of the will of a small community—a caste or a stratum of the population or a racial group—which in its turn behaves like a violent individual towards other, and perhaps more numerous, collections of people.[37]

That statement has an intellectually challenging coda: "the liberty of the individual is no gift of civilization." In Freud's terms, civilization was by definition opposed to human freedom. It was the source of inhibition, not "development." Men and women instinctively through sexual love cause new difficulties in every generation for the state that wishes to perpetuate itself. These men and women do not work through civilization but often against it. *Civilization and Its Discontents* concludes by observing that states want unity, while individuals want happiness. Under such circumstances, the "developmental process of the individual" cannot be expected to attain those benefits that we associate with progress.

I have referred to a number of writers who read the literature of the decade as it appeared—and to some who affected that literature before it appeared. Isaiah Berlin is in the first category. He was not the greatest philosopher of midcentury, but he was the philosopher who wrote most to the point about what was being done and thought. Berlin was especially skeptical of categorical theory, and his work ranks high among the great critiques of progress and perfectibility. Walter Lippmann and George Santayana read and sometimes wrote, consciously, about the same subjects that novelists did. They are primary sources for the meanings of terms and ideas. One cannot proceed in the study of the twenties without understanding the refractive powers of Bertrand Russell. The greatest of its philosophers was, of course, Ludwig Wittgenstein, who gave to writers their language of thought about being. I have been drawn to Freud's writings on culture more often than to those on human sexuality (given the difficulty of separating the subjects in his work). My overarching subjects have been the ways in which moderns thought about thinking and the language in which their arguments were conducted.

1
Fitzgerald and the Geography of Progress

We see the connected and opposed regions of North and South in many of Fitzgerald's stories and novels: "The Ice Palace" (May 1920), "The Jelly-Bean" (October 1920), "Two For a Cent" (April 1922), "The Diamond as Big as the Ritz" (June 1922), *The Beautiful and Damned* (1922), "Dice, Brassknuckles & Guitar" (May 1923), "The Third Casket" (May 1924), "The Sensible Thing" (July 1924), *The Great Gatsby* (1925), "The Dance" (June 1926), "The Last of the Belles" (March 1929), "Basil and Cleopatra" (April 1929), "Two Wrongs" (January 1930), "Flight And Pursuit" (May 1932), "Family in the Wind" (June 1932).[1] Simply by recalling the tenor of these works we can begin to understand their thematic importance. There is, clearly, a *modern* conflict between North and South.[2] The War between the States takes on contemporary shape in these works. The new war involves our national character and purpose. It sets certain traditional values against those of progress and success. We are intended to rethink—as Fitzgerald himself did—not only our Victorian past but historical time itself.

There were a number of American Dreams in the twenties, and Robert Nisbet reminds us that some of them had a theology: "Faith in mankind's advance to an even better future assumed the same kind of evangelical zeal, especially among the American masses, that is associated with religion."[3] That seems to be accurate—we recall that *The Rise of American Civilization* had in 1927 connected our "invulnerable faith" in the means of technology to the end of "unlimited progress."[4] Nisbet, like Charles A. and Mary R. Beard, reminds us that our native, material version of the Idea of Progress was not killed off by the Great War. In fact, it was "never more compelling than during the first four or five decades of the twentieth century."[5] Not everyone agreed with this variant of civic religion. Yet, despite the satire of writers like H. L. Mencken and Sinclair Lewis, it was indeed conventional to think that prosperity incarnated the Idea of Progress.

F. Scott Fitzgerald was among those who took the notion with a grain of salt. We think almost automatically of Gatsby presiding over his transformation, looking first at the windows of his palace and then at every one of his doors and towers and counting the years it took to buy them. But property offers the same problem to literature as to philosophy. Towns, buildings, and markets are ephemeral. They inevitably become reminders of material limits. The same images used by advertisers to celebrate growth were used by writers of the twenties to reverse the common judgment about it. Van Wyck Brooks wrote about pioneer cities no longer populated, ghost towns "all but obliterated in alkali dust." Fitzgerald wrote about the entropic ruins of the American landscape in the village of Fish and the Valley of Ashes.[6] He often used architectonic images—arrogant towers, faded mansions, bungalow tracts crawling along farm fields, even one particular broken-down billboard—to suggest defeated *national* expectations. These things were, after all, imagery in the public realm.[7]

There is in Fitzgerald not only an idea of but a geography of progress. When Nick Carraway organizes Gatsby's funeral, he asks Mr. Gatz if he "might want to take the body west." But the answer is that "Jimmy always liked it better down East."[8] Both remarks need their context. Fitzgerald's description of America rests on a real and also metaphorical sense of geography. As to the first, his map consists of familiar quadrants: North, South, East, and West. As to the second, East and North, conventionally the same, are poised against West—and especially against South. The East opposes other regions and is understood in relation to them. That should be factored into our understanding of passages that seem confined to geographical meanings. Here, for example, is Tom Buchanan on New York:

"Oh, I'll stay in the East, don't you worry," he said, glancing at Daisy and then back at me as if he were alert for something more. "I'd be a God Damn fool to live anywhere else." (12)

On the face of it this is unmysterious, conveying information the same way Mr. Gatz does when he tells Nick that Jimmy "rose up to his position in the East" (131). But Tom both asserts and conceals. He is from monied Chicago—and H. L. Mencken had just written that rich men come from "the fat lands of the Middle West" to New York because "the ordinary American law does not run there."[9] Mencken is not referring solely to the Volstead Act; his essay is about sexual opportunism in commercial form. In Mencken, Metropolis is a marketplace of commodities, including things human. "There is little in New York," he writes in another essay of 1927, "that does not spring from money."[10] It is reasonably plain in *The Great Gatsby* that Tom's affair with Myrtle is a transaction. Myrtle knows a lot about price and marketplace values. She despises her husband for having borrowed a suit for their wedding, falls in love, in part, with Tom's own shoes and suit and high style, uses his money to transform her own social class from blue-collar to bourgeois. Myrtle knows about two subjects important to Mencken and to his theme: everything is for sale, and "most of these fellas will cheat you every time" (27). Cheating is the essential mode of capitalism in Mencken's New York essays. He provides a long catalog of terms like "exploiter," "merchants," "customer," "sharper," and "bawds and pimps," which define each other while defining the economy. Notably, he writes about bootlegging as the central "industry" of Metropolis.[11] The East, the home of progress, embodies serious contradictions.

Fitzgerald wrote that his story "May Day" shows his attempt to "weave . . . into a pattern" his experience of living in New York.[12] The meaning of that pattern is displayed in the story's opening—and is reinforced by ideas in circulation at the time. New York is the incarnation of marketplace values that are "hymned by the scribes and poets" of advertising (98). We know that writers resisted the confusion of progress with prosperity. They were not satisfied by industrial democracy and resented its commercialism. More than anything, they resented its claims. Toward the end of the decade, in *A Preface to Morals,* Walter Lippmann stated that the theory of "mechanical progress" was the latest false religion.[13] Lewis Mumford located this inflation of values in New York, which was the East incarnate: "Broadway, in sum, is the façade of the American city: a false front. The highest achievements of our material civilization—and at their best our hotels, our department stores, and our Woolworth towers are achievements—count as so many symptoms of its spiritual failure. In order to cover up the vacancy of getting and spending in our cities, we have invented a thousand fresh devices for getting and spending. As a consequence our life is externalized."[14]

Fitzgerald's writings of the early twenties invoke "devices for getting and spending" in the form of advertised commodities.[15] Artifacts appear everywhere in the fiction, like these from "The Last of the Belles": "I stumbled here and there in the knee-deep underbrush, looking for my youth in a clapboard or a strip of roofing or a rusty tomato can" (462). Roland Marchand's *Advertising the American Dream* remarks of copy text and image that such objects had already entered the nation's visual vocabulary in the twenties. To refer to them is to refer to the vast and necessarily false metonym of progress. When that tomato can had first been described, it was in the language of superlatives and even adulation; it meant future satisfaction and not only in a material way.[16] Fitzgerald's extraordinary images of decay in the public realm constitute a formidable argument against progress. Marchand identifies the imagery of the *new* with a social apologetic:

> Civilization . . . had found a way to regain Nature's intended gifts without sacrificing the fruits of progress. . . . In proclaiming the victories over threats to health and beauty that the products of civilization now made possible, these parables of Civilization Redeemed never sought to denigrate Nature. . . . Civilization, which had brought down the curse of Nature upon itself, had still proved capable of discovering products that would enable Nature's original and beneficent intentions to triumph. . . . the advance of civilization . . . need never exact any real losses. Civilization had become its own redeemer.[17]

Fitzgerald has his own notion of civilization, expressed by contravening images. In "The Ice Palace" we see colors "of light gold and dark gold and shiny red" dominating the Bellamy library. These are the colors of money and desire. But the books appear to be unread—they are objects and artifacts, as in the later scene of Jay Gatsby's own library. The more important point is the opposition of cost and value in the Bellamy household, a place specifically identified with cost and value in the North. Unmediated wealth has accumulated only "a lot of fairly expensive things . . . that all looked about fifteen years old" (56). These commodities have no past—which makes them perfect objective correlatives for wealth without history, that is, for progress without meaning.

Because the North is where progress happens, it is bound to display the uneasy connection between prosperity and progress. Fitzgerald disputes that connection repeatedly. In his fiction, "success" involuntarily aspires to a higher, moralized form of itself. Even the provincial Mr. Gatz believes that his son would "of helped build up the country" (131) if he had lived. Our civic religion holds that the accumulated sum of individual successes adds up to national progress. This was the promise of the North. But, even in the South, our duty is to change and improve.

Fitzgerald's stories about the South point out the failure of unaided "tradition." The mention of that phrase in the twenties assumes the need to recall and even to embody the past. Yet, in Fitzgerald's South, evolution is imperative: the Jelly-bean realizes that he has to "make somethin'" out of his farm and his life (157); Sally Carrol Happer explains that she needs "to live where things happen" (51). Sara Haardt, who grew up in Montgomery with Zelda Sayre, understood the necessity for change—or at least of escape: "Oh, no use talking, the South was sweet. But it was a sweetness tinged with the melancholy of death. It was because beauty, somehow, is shorter lived in the South than in the North, or in the West; and beauty, more than mere survival, is the most poignant proof of life."[18] In "The Ice Palace" Fitzgerald dealt with this conception through the idea of the *vita activa*. Evanescence was the field of vitality.

"Dice, Brassknuckles & Guitar" is a regional parable of the early twenties. Its central figure, Jim Powell, is southern, romantic, chivalrous, unsophisticated. He sees things with great clarity but no perspective. Jim is on his way north to the land of money and opportunity. Equipped with the kinds of knowledge implied by the story's title, he is innocent of the knowledge of how the social world works. By the end of the story he offends his wealthy patrons, is put in his place, and then is forced to leave. Present works against past in this story, as city works against province. Fitzgerald's language dwells insistently on "Victorian" qualities of character, mind, and landscape. He was of two minds about the meaning of that phrase. It could mean what Wells, Shaw, and Strachey intended it to mean, serving as a synonym for outmoded ideas. But it also meant a connection to time, place, and even to one's own beginnings: "here and there lie patches of garden country dotted with old-fashioned frame mansions, which have wide shady porches and a red swing on the lawn. And perhaps, on the widest and shadiest of the porches there is even a hammock left over from the hammock days, stirring gently in a mid-Victorian wind." The passing tourist "can't see the hammock from the road—but sometimes there's a girl in the hammock" (237). In this story the term "Victorian" does not suggest repressiveness. The opposite is suggested, as if the past had something to offer at least as important as "the twentieth century" did. There is in fact a girl in the hammock; her name, Amanthis, connotes (according to the *Oxford English Dictionary*) both love and belief. The text argues through images. It tells us not only that she has wonderful yellow hair but that "there was something enormously yellow about the whole scene" (238). The language offers a prevision of the yellow and gold in *The Great Gatsby,* colors that symbolize promise. But the Victorian scene cannot contain those feelings generated within it. Amanthis is attracted to Jim Powell, who brings to the monied North a sense of style and idea long since forgotten. But he is disarmed by his innocence, and she by her sophistication. He will return to the ever more eccentric South; she will become part of the ever more progressive North. A sleeping beauty quite literally awakens in this story, but Harold Lloyd is in a role that needs Tyrone Power.

In "The Ice Palace" Sally Carrol Happer has her own "awakening." Both stories begin with real and figurative possibilities. In Fitzgerald, the idea of "beginning" often needs to be qualified because an opening may be a continuation of history: "The sunlight dripped over the house like golden paint over an art jar, and the freckling shadows here and there only intensified the rigor of the bath of light. Up in her bedroom window Sally Carrol Happer rested her nineteen-year-old chin on a fifty-two-year old sill" (48). It seems unlikely that "Life in Tarleton, Georgia, after all, nurtured only the most negative aspects of romantic egotism." Nor do I think that such passages are meant to be viewed under the aspect of Tennyson's "Lotos-Eaters."[19] The argument that the South was an example of *cultural* enervation was commonplace enough before Fitzgerald's story appeared, but it took a different slant. The region was agrarian in an industrial age and fundamentalist in an age of skepticism. As seen by H. L. Mencken the South had no textual culture: its poets, historians, and novelists were simply a national joke. But Fitzgerald was not much concerned with Baptist morality or with literary amateurism.[20] To worry about those things was to confuse ideas with essences.

Fitzgerald's southern characters are important because their minds and manners have been shaped by time and place. In the first part of "The Ice Palace" time is more than referential; it is a protagonist. Sally Carrol Happer keeps returning to the graveyard in Tarleton because it is history objectified. Like Fitzgerald himself, she is of two minds about past and present. She knows how important it is to use her energies, to operate within the realm of material substance. She is not an innocent and knows that money and power are the means of life. But she also values the style of life that understands money and power to be means and not ends. She is an idealist, and Santayana had observed in 1920 that American idealism is material to the extent that it "goes hand in hand with present contentment and with foresight of what the future very likely will actually bring."[21] That idealism wants to work, achieve, produce. As Sally Carrol puts the issue, the "sort of energy" she has "may be useful somewhere" (51). Energy needs a field of action, and the North provides that. But without the past, Santayana writes, Americans could have no "fixity in human morals, in institutions, or in ideas." Necessarily (and we think of Fitzgerald's invocations of "Victorian" permanence and southern stasis), "*America is full of mitigations of Americanism.* There are survivals; there are revolts; there is a certain hesitation in the main current itself, carrying the nation towards actions and sentiments not altogether congruous with experimental progress."[22] His conclusion applies to Sally Carrol Happer and also to Charlie Wales in "Babylon Revisited," who "wanted to jump back a whole generation" (619). As Stanley Brodwin put it, certain of Fitzgerald's stories show "the tension between living presence and its gift of ontological triumph through a past, lost moment of history on the one hand and ongoing personal experience on the other."[23]

The South is more than "a warm, pleasant, and lazy place, a home of good manners and elegant traditions, a garden which, for Fitzgerald, grew Southern belles and jelly-beans."[24] The South must mean more than that if only because *it exists in relation to the North.* In making a point about dominant national values, Milton R. Stern observes that the worship of industriousness had been corrupted: "ideologies of work, responsibility, politeness, respect, decency, had been perverted and bastardized" in the pursuit of wealth. These, I think, are northern virtues, and they have remade the nation. If they prove false, then there is not much leverage for criticism of the South because the connection between regions is dialectical.

Stern's comment on Fitzgerald—that he "chooses community and history"[25]—is worth recalling. Such choice was difficult: in 1922, Harold E. Stearns began *Civilization in the United States* with the argument that "We have no heritages or traditions to which to cling except those that have already withered in our hands and turned to dust."[26] That, essentially, is the problem posed by Fitzgerald's stories about the conflictual relationship of North and South, or of progress and tradition. It may be that *both* progress and tradition are fictions. Cleanth Brooks writes that there are really two myths of American history. One of these is the idea of the Old South, rooted gracefully in time. The other is the idea of the New North, advancing into the future: "If there is a myth of the Southern past, we must recognize that there is a myth of the American future—its more respectable name is the American Dream—and with reference to the charge that the Southern myth erred in describing its past as golden, one might point out that the American myth has consistently insisted that its future was made of the same precious metal."[27] Fitzgerald seems to have understood that one myth of American life might be no more convincing than the other. He was not engaged by the northern ideology, which he knew differed greatly from its material forms. In 1923, he stated that Chicago and St. Paul had "wealth without background, tradition, or manners."[28] Just before this, in 1922, he had described the Southern "tradition of before-the-war culture" with this summary phrase: "most of which is false."[29]

Two of Fitzgerald's stories of the early twenties suggest southern "community and history" in terms of opposed ideas. The first of these stories, "Two For A Cent," refers itself to those golden colors of *The Great Gatsby* and of the primeval South: A yellow sky is seen by a man sitting on "an immemorial bench, for the sky was every shade of yellow, the color of tan, the color of gold, the color of peaches." The view of red buildings and yellow sky "was beautiful" and like a "dream."[30] Fitzgerald customarily thinks in colors, and we know that these colors mattered to him. But against the new-world colors of the horizon are human facts. Fitzgerald, who takes the idea of community literally, may have more to say about houses than Jane Austen. In the new South, "Bungalows . . . were reproducing their species . . . as though by some monstrous affiliation with the guinea-pig; it was the most common type of house in the country. It was a house built by a race whose more energetic complement hoped either to move up or move on" (34). The last line identifies the northern style of energy and progress without direction as it has come unbidden to Fitzgerald's "immemorial" South.

In at least one case, Fitzgerald arrived at a compromise. Fittingly enough, it is stated in a form bordering on fantasy. His story "The Third Casket" follows (at a distance) act 1 of *The Merchant of Venice*. In Shakespeare, Portia is advised that "Your father was ever virtuous, and holy men at their death have good inspirations; therefore the lottery that he hath devised in these three chests of gold, silver, and lead, whereof who chooses his meaning chooses you, will no doubt never be chosen by any rightly but one who you shall rightly love."[31] Fitzgerald paid a good deal of attention to this passage but even more to a certain interpretation of its meaning.

"The Third Casket" has something to do with the inheriting daughter, Lola, but is in fact about her father, Cyrus Girard, a worried Wall Street broker of sixty who seems singularly free of any good inspirations. He offers his business and his daughter to the one of three men who does the best job of making money. The story rests—uncomfortably—on myth and fantasy: as Girard puts it, the winner will get what fairy tales give, "half my kingdom and, if she wants him, my daughter's hand" (88). So far, the story is an approximation of Portia's story and of those tales located on the unseen edges of *The Great Gatsby*. But dividing up a kingdom ought to give us a different kind of clue. This is not wholly about *The Merchant of Venice* nor wholly about Shakespeare.

Fitzgerald's title comes from Freud's recent essay "The Theme of the Three Caskets," which had memorably been applied to *King Lear*.[32] In *King Lear* and in Fitzgerald's story we see an old man perilously close to dying unregenerate. And, as Freud states of that tragedy, "the relationship of a father to his children, which might be a fruitful source of many dramatic situations, is not turned to further account."[33] Nor is it here. Fitzgerald's Portia has only a minor role; the old man is on center stage. His fate is the issue. Nothing in *The Merchant of Venice* corresponds to Fitzgerald's plot, which begins with an old man saying that Americans don't know what to do with their lives. The middle of the story is about middle age, the end about the coming of death. These are in fact the death themes of Freud's essay. He saw in the scene of choosing three daughters or "caskets" a way of understanding the ordinary conditions of life: "A choice is made where in reality there is obedience to a compulsion." That is to say, in choosing what is most humble, and what most resembles a leaden coffin, death is "recognized intellectually."[34] The father comes to terms with reality in Freud and also in Fitzgerald. His story is their plot.

There are other themes common to Freud and to Fitzgerald. According to the former, "King Lear's dramatic story" shows "that one should not give up one's possessions and rights during one's lifetime."[35] But I think the main connection resides in Cyrus Girard's awareness that "fairy tales" may after all correspond to life. Freud's essay refers particularly to Cinderella, the stories of Paris and of Psyche, and "The Twelve Brothers" and "The Six Swans" of the Brothers Grimm. They are all fables of loss and regeneration, important for Freud's argument of symbolic representation.

Fitzgerald's own fable in the stories I have listed was the mystical marriage of North and South. It was clearly one way of looking at his divided American allegiances, at his own marriage, and at the romantic tensions of his novels and stories. There are too many North-South oppositions to disregard. In certain of his stories, a marriage fails to take place, which remains to the narrator a lifelong matter of regret. In "The Last of the Belles" the narrator has to give up not only on the girl but on the place that the South, which is the past itself, can retain in his memory. As noted, most of its traditions "are false." In certain other stories a marriage does take place but, as in "The Sensible Thing," unsolvable ambiguities remain. In the case of "The Third Casket," possibly to no one's surprise, the successful suitor is from the South. He has that largeness of character denied to his rivals, and he convinces both father and daughter that the Wall Street firm is better off when managed by someone who comes from outside "the most hard-boiled commercial age any country ever knew" (90). Just after Girard realizes how old he is, he gets renewed life—"twenty good years"—from his discovery of the virtues of the southern candidate. Both convince each other: the old man from the North admits that profit needs values, while his new partner and son-in-law admits that values need work. As a story, it is deeply unsatisfactory. The characters are there only in charcoal outline. But an idea that Fitzgerald took seriously is not obscured by trivialities of form.

In "Basil and Cleopatra" the Civil War is fought again, although when history repeats itself it takes the form of farce, with Littleboy Le Moyne disappearing under a pile of Yankee bodies at the battle of New Haven. When the South comes North in *The Great Gatsby*, we see a realistic per-mutation in the relationship of "innocent" Louisville and New York. In "The Third Casket," in which North also marries South, a consummation occurs that in other stories may often be wished but never happens. This is a coda to all those other narratives in which the history of the republic is left as it actually was. The marriage of North and South is considerably more than a convenience of plot for Fitzgerald, and it speaks to more than his own marriage. It says a good deal about his view of American history, a history of alienation and disunion that mirrored and perhaps explained his sense of self. By far the majority of North-South marriages in Fitzgerald don't work or simply remain imperfect. This repeated story was useful in more than one way for Fitzgerald: as a revelation of his personal experience and also as an encoded representation of his sense of history. It is not a matter of correcting history through fiction. Freud's essay concludes—somewhat doctrinally—that art tries "to satisfy the wishes that reality does not satisfy."[36] That is usually the path not taken by Fitzgerald. From time to time he will think about themes of congruence and even of regeneration. But, in most cases, his map of the American scene is faithful to reality and not to wishes.

2
Hemingway and "the New America"

Hemingway often displaces personal with national identity: "American women" in "The Short Happy Life of Francis Macomber"; "the American and the girl with him" in "Hills Like White Elephants"; "the American lady" (and the elaborate sequence of "American" references) in "A Canary for One." There are "American tales" that seem by definition untrue in "Banal Story." And there are recurrent appearances—the provincial-minded Old Lady in *Death in the Afternoon,* the New York Princetonian Robert Cohn in *The Sun Also Rises*—of characters whose Americanism means limits of mind and sensibility. The assessment of Americanism was a crowded field from just before the twenties to just after the thirties. And, as Walter Lippmann wrote in 1929, Hemingway was clearly an important judge of national character, especially of its failings.[1]

There was much to work with: *America's Coming-Of-Age* by Van Wyck Brooks (1915) is a revisionist view of the qualities of the "American Mind."[2] Mencken's "The Sahara of the Bozart" (1917) began a series of essays on politics, manners, and our intellectual life. Brooks's *Letters and Leadership* (1918) added some thunderous criticism both of "Old America" and also of "Young America," which needed definitive new ideas to go along with its new sense of self. George Santayana's *Character and Opinion in the United States* appeared in 1920. In 1922, *Civilization in the United States* featured essays on "The City" by Lewis Mumford, "Scholarship and

Criticism" by Joel Spingarn, "The Intellectual Life" by Harold E. Stearns (who edited the entire collection), "Poetry" by Conrad Aiken, "History" by Hendrik Willem Van Loon—and a self-conscious selection of essays on "American Civilization from the Foreign Point of View." That was also the year of Lippmann's *Public Opinion*. In 1925, the Modern Library edition of William James appeared, with a section headed "The American Scene." Charles A. and Mary R. Beard produced *The Rise of American Civilization* in 1927. Santayana's "The Genteel Tradition at Bay" appeared in 1931. This is to say little of the extraordinary coverage of national life and ideas by Sinclair Lewis in *Babbitt,* Scott Fitzgerald in his three novels of the early twenties, and Hemingway in his two novels of the later twenties. The analysis of American ideas, ideals, and manners had become a genre. Hemingway seems to have understood the situation perfectly: Harold E. Stearns appears briefly as Harvey Stone in *The Sun Also Rises* in order to inform us how wrong Mencken has turned out to be, while Donald Ogden Stewart, a model for Bill Gorton, had published *A Parody Outline of History* (1921), whose subtitle promised "an amusing and satirical picture of American letters of today."[3] In any case, a mind acquainted with both Ezra Pound and Gertrude Stein could not have passed a day in Paris without responding to ideas about the making of Americans.[4]

It has been noted that the unnamed "Americans of 'Out of Season' lack both a cohesive sense of time and a language in which to express its loss."[5] More than one kind of time is involved, and more than one sense of definition. As in other references to Americans in Hemingway, recurrence defines. The story repeats Peduzzi's phrase "young gentleman" so often (more than thirty times) that it becomes a dominant idea as well as a statistic. Why is the phrase there? One possibility is that it shows the mentality of the man using it—and the story is for the most part told from his point of view. So reiteration implies the limits of a character who can think only within given categories. But that can't be the main reason for Hemingway's heavy investment in repetition. After some thirty restatements the phrase becomes the most visible bloc of language in the story. It becomes as much of a quantity as, say, a sequence of related images. It may appear in all its manifold locations in order to say *more* than Peduzzi can. The evidence for knowing "what other people think" has recently been summarized by Donald Davidson, our leading philosopher of language: "we observe their acts, read their letters, study their expressions, listen to their words, learn their histories, and note their relations to society. . . . Sometimes I learn what I believe in much the same way someone else does, by noticing what I say."[6]

We begin to understand Peduzzi through that repeated phrase and to sense his inability to see past it into the actual personality of its subject. Finally, we begin to use that phrase ourselves. The many recurrences force us to become aware of multiple meanings. The husband in the story is seen as a "young gentleman" by a man familiar with the locution but not its meaning. The same may be said about the subject of the locution. The technique is awkwardly indirect, but say this for drunken servile ignorance—the phrase gets to overshadow the story. It works *because* it is wrong, suggesting fake gentility and an acquired sense of self. And, of course, it means that gentility itself may be faked. The monotonous reuse of the phrase lets into the story the contempt that Hemingway has for the ideas behind it. That attitude was not idiosyncratic—Mencken's *The American Language* states that there was an aspect of "masquerade" about our national euphemisms for gentility. Britons scrutinize the application of "gentleman" more carefully than we do, making sure that "the man referred to is always actually a gentleman by their standards."[7] The British-American contrast (frequent in Hemingway) is applied by Jake Barnes to Robert Cohn in the second chapter of *The Sun Also Rises.* Cohn mistakenly admires the "perfect English gentleman" conjured up by W. H. Hudson's *The Purple Land* and, even more mistakenly, seems to believe that he can become such a figure himself. That phrase "gentleman" will refer itself to other imitative Americans.

Misapplied by Peduzzi, the term lets us see into the pretense of character and class. The dialogue of this story is famously impervious. Much is left to the reader's interpretation. But when we see that "young gentleman" without the will or style to go back to the hotel or dodge Peduzzi, or pay the right amount for anything, or state the thing that either does or does not make a difference, then the rest of his dialogue also is devalued. He seems not to know about manner or style, although Peduzzi thanks him in a large way for a small tip, "in the tone of one member of the Carleton Club accepting the *Morning Post* from another."[8] Inference and parallelism go beyond a transaction that defines by what it misses.

Hemingway has a clear conception of the real thing. In the seventh chapter of *The Sun Also Rises* the Count, Jake, and Brett have a series of dialogues about food, wine, business, war, and "values." They go to a restaurant in the Bois, one of the rare places in the novel where the word "good" is used for anything. Given its associations—it is the great descriptive of Genesis—that word is not handled lightly by Hemingway. There has been prior thought about establishing authenticity. The first information to reach us comes from Jake's concierge. She is one of many functionaries in Hemingway whose business is to tell us about protagonists. The concierge first quantifies then qualifies—the transference by parallelism is ingenious. Brett has been to Jake's flat, accompanied by a man who "was very large. Very, very large. She was very nice. Very, very nice." The point is then elaborated: "I'll speak perfectly frankly, Monsieur Barnes. Last night I found her not so gentille. Last night I formed another idea of her. But listen to what I tell you. She is très, très gentille. She is of very good family. It is a thing you can see."[9] There are ambiguities because, although this concierge's life work is detecting the socially true from the false, not every diagnosis works. One may need some kind of passport— and Brett has slipped her two hundred francs, which might put anyone in the *Almanach de Gotha*. More ambiguities: the money comes from the count. But the main point is made: Brett has an identity strong enough to register even though it may lie somewhere between the ideal and Robert Cohn's sense of it.

Certain British figures—Brett, Wilson in "The Short Happy Life of Francis Macomber"—do not live up to standards but express them decisively. Americans like Macomber or Robert Cohn are evaluated against them. At one point, Brett says to Jake of Cohn's exhausting pursuit that "He did behave badly" (143). The phrase has a long afterlife: "He's behaved very badly. . . . Damned badly. . . . Nobody else would behave as badly. . . . Everybody behaves badly. . . . You wouldn't behave badly" (181). The irony is more extensive than appears because if facts have no moral definition in life then what remains is style—that is to say, the way that amoral fact is experienced.

When we encounter an "American lady" in "A Canary for One" we see in a diminished way Americanism as a style. The story runs a close second to "Out of Season" in its replications—there are more than twenty refer-

ences to "the American lady" plus a number of allusions to American husbands, children—and what might be called false truisms. "The American
lady" explains in more detail than is needed how she acquired the canary—
her recall of the transaction is apologetic, explanatory, anxious. A second
allusion suggests fussiness and, again, a kind of diminution of manner to
say nothing of mind. She walks, talks, reads aimlessly and worries about
missing the train. When the train moves, she fears that it's going too fast;
at night she stays awake expecting a train wreck (338). It seems from our
own viewpoint in the twenty-first century to be a case of anxiety well
observed—but "nerves" were then associated with more than psychology.
Civilization in the United States (1922) has a chapter on the subject, which
begins by stating that "Young enough as America is, she is nevertheless old
enough to have known the time when there was no such things as nerves."
These belong "to our age of indulgence and luxury"—that is to say, the
twenties.[10]

The phrase "American lady" in this story is as equivocal as "young
gentleman" in "Out of Season." The first time we see either phrase we give
credence to denoted meanings. When reiterated the four terms in these
two phrases accrue other meanings. In *The American Language,* Mencken
points out that the word "lady" used to be "the English euphemism-of-all-
work." However, "in the United States *lady* is definitely out of favor" because it does not reflect modern actualities.[11] Its use reveals an attitude but
not a condition. There may be ladies still in view (Hemingway believes in
them if not in gents), yet the term itself is suspect. The narrator of "A
Canary for One" establishes something when he uses the term; it is subject
to all the ambiguities of honorifics.

Quite soon the term "lady" will poison the term "American." Its subject
begins to deliver unverifiable opinions about the superiority of American
husbands. These seem to assert the virtues of our national character, but
context works against statement. It is a problem of language, what Isaiah
Berlin described as the effect of saying familiar things in ways that alter the
meaning of words. The concepts are twisted "in such a fashion that they
produce an electrifying effect upon the reader, who is insensibly drawn by
the familiar expressions into wholly unfamiliar country."[12] The assertions
must be set against the qualities of her own husband, which in the text—
hence in reality—are nonexistent, and against those of "a man in Vevey"

who falls short of those nonexistent qualities. Perhaps, not being in the story, they have no being at home or in history. The phrase "husband" is more complex than it appears in Hemingway's life and work.

"My little girl"—a reiterated phrase with changing meanings—is now momentarily a woman. Words tend at this point to mean something other than what they say, as in "no foreigner can make an American girl a good husband." We understand that such a statement requires translation. Distancing implies attitudes and even hatreds. Part of the phrase may have no connection at all to its object. Certain words in this story have a very short life span: the daughter regresses to being a "girl," the man has become a "foreigner."[13] The description of "a good husband" particularly invites interpretation. It may not be a real category because there isn't anyone who can fit the definition. "The American lady"—can she be America herself?—represents the kind of thinking Lippmann described, an interpretation of reality disconnected from real things.

Back to issues palpably on her mind—clothing for sale at a maison de couture in the Rue Saint Honoré. There is an excruciating intrusion into the story of a second narrative describing how her purchases are measured, made, shipped, and opened. We get information that we do not necessarily want about their passage through customs and about the "vendeuse, named Amélie" who has been helpful (340). Hemingway uses the two levels of discourse as he does in "Out of Season": the subject becomes known by its object. Donald Davidson puts the matter this way: "this raises the question what sort of relations we or our minds are thought to have to these objects when we say they are before our mind."[14] A state of mind is determined by its view, and the view tells us quite a lot about the viewer.[15] Our critical problem in this story is the relationship of mind to its subject. The subject will turn out to be greater than we may think, the mind much less.

Information and inference are buried, as they are intended to be, in the detail of the American lady's own narrative: the daughter won't need to ask for changes in size because she is "grown up" now. She seems, however, not to know that she is grown up and neither does her mother. As in "Out of Season," misinformation clarifies. We hear again, insistently, that American men make the best husbands. This may or not be a true statement, but it does reveal truths. The most interesting of them may not be what the statement says but rather what it means. According to Davidson, "all propositional attitudes exhibit first person authority. . . . Belief and desire are relatively clear and simple examples." He adds that "Error is possible; so is doubt."[16] The story seems to illustrate his reasoning: from this point on the relationship of statement to fact weakens. Davidson's analysis of the language of perception raises an especially important point, one of his best-known statements on the problem of meaning: "In communication, what a speaker and the speaker's interpreter must share is an understanding of what the speaker means by what he says."[17] This is a very far-reaching conclusion, and it has not made the philosophy of language any less complex. So far as the story is concerned, its assertions are in doubt: any given number of them may not be true. We are not much concerned with Americans being better husbands, something that can be guessed but not proven. But we are concerned with what the assertion may indicate about the person making it and, of course, with beliefs reported as facts, prejudices stated as reasons—and reasons disguised by language.

A much larger issue is only gradually revealed: we don't know what love means, either in relation to the daughter or as an American conception. Are we missing something here? The daughter's symptoms of grief are perceived by a mind that does not want to credit them. They may be as trivial as they look (although in other historical times such symptoms would have been taken seriously). They are a suspiciously consistent match to the daughter's description by her mother. But even in the modernizing twenties the reader knows what meanings are inscribed in love. George Santayana's *Reason in Society* (reprinted 1919) is a compendium of ideas, some of which will strike us as being surprisingly contemporary. Santayana is sympathetic to sexual love. He posits a hidden, hostile relationship between love and the middle-class mind. He warns that the superficially reasonable and even sympathetic discussion of sexual love may have altogether a different agenda: the "formalism natural to language" easily disguises hatred. It is not the direct attack against which one is *en garde* but the apologetic reconstruction of reality. According to Santayana's idea of language, we intuit anger—even rage—from "an insistence on reticence and hypocrisy.[18] That does put another face on the discussion by one person of another's experience.

What is the relationship of the experience to its description? The sufferings of the daughter are seen only through the narration of the mother. The symptoms that the American lady describes set the affair within the limited emotional range of adolescence—even of childhood. The description is intended to diminish the seriousness of the love experience undergone. The American lady's selective description is intended to prevent interpretation. It certainly expresses the moralized hostility to love that Santayana thought characteristic of the American mind. Is the affair as trivial as the symptoms seem to be? There is, after all, a second love story in the narrative and, although that story too is never directly voiced, we give it our credence. It may be far more important than the story we have heard. But it necessarily shares operative terminology with the first story told by the American lady. So the terms "American," "lady," "good," and "husband" become equivocal as they are examined. There seems to be no bedrock beneath our surface.

⮠

In 1930, Hemingway told Max Perkins that his work had been badly misunderstood by Edmund Wilson. This evolved into a position not only on critics and criticism but on the act of explanation itself:

> There has never been a word written in criticism or explanation of Miss Gertrude Stein's, or Mr. James Joyce's work which was not a reflection of a derivation of something explained by Miss Stein or Mr. Joyce to some critic in conversation. All interpretation of what they have done, explanations and glorifications, have originated with the writers themselves. This does not detract from the value of their work per se but it is some thing which would make the practice of letters unbearable to me. I do not explain because of some noble virtue you see in myself nor [ ] the friendship of critics but only because to do so would make writing not worth doing and all together disgusting. Writing is made to be read; the writer should keep out of it. If he explains something into it which is not there, it will only lose in the End.[19]

Hemingway was especially concerned with the intellectual tic of explaining the inexplicable. He associated that with the literature of midcult, and in one of his stories on American mental life he attacked that mode with heavy satire.

Hemingway's Americans have a certain style or absence of it. There are some caveats—it is good to learn about his personal manner, but I don't believe that "the [sartorial] style Hemingway helped establish became the primary American visual image for rejecting aristocratic notions of elegance, opulence, leisure. . . . "[20] In other words, he dressed as he thought— a conclusion beyond proof. More importantly, Hemingway did not reject those "notions." In fact, he admired them. Here is Jake Barnes on the embodiment of style in language, with an explicit contrast of cultures:

> When you were with English you got into the habit of using English expressions in your thinking. The English spoken language—the upper classes, anyway—must have fewer words than the Eskimo. Of course I didn't know anything about the Eskimo . . . The English talked with inflected phrases. One phrase to mean everything. I liked them though. I liked the way they talked. (149)

The phrase describes Jake Barnes, but Fitzgerald thought that Hemingway himself liked the way the English talked.[21] He also liked the way they thought. Manner, he thought, was not only a way of doing things but of setting up barriers, of doing them in the one way that was right— sometimes, of not doing them at all. In his work, rules that come from somewhere govern eating, drinking, and hunting—things stylistically larger than they seem to be. The rules do not simply prohibit the shooting of lions from moving cars.[22] In *The Sun Also Rises* they govern life in both Paris and Pamplona. Infractions bring penalties: the loss of friendship or self-respect. These penalties are never made up; things are never restored. Little in Hemingway escapes judgment: Nick Adams thinks about humping cans of beans and spaghetti into camp and says, "I've got a right to eat this kind of stuff, if I'm willing to carry it" (215). He is in the middle of nowhere when he says that, but he does have a historical witness: Fernand Braudel's essay "Superfluity and Sufficiency" points out that thought about personal style is "an indication of deeper phenomena."[23] He concludes, in fact, that opinion about "food, drink, housing, clothes and fashion" is an important aspect of, even an expression of, supposedly higher thought. What we call civilization is composed of "strange collections of commodities, symbols, illusions, fantasms and intellectual schema."[24] In *The Sun Also Rises* there are two reasonably reliable witnesses, Jake Barnes and the

Count, who speak for the construction of values. While they address small things *it is always clear that larger issues are implied:* there are in fact "mysteries of manners, arms, and arts."[25] Robert Cohn does not understand that; the Count and Jake do.

Hemingway's "Banal Story" goes directly and without the modulation of dialogue into the connection between style and mind. It begins with a satirical description of the authors, critics, and writers of the *Forum* magazine.[26] In 1925 the editor of this magazine, Henry Goddard Leach, had stated that it was intended "to Interpret the New America That Is Attaining National Consciousness in the Decade in which We Live."[27] It is a gem of pomposity. The issue is not so much the reduction of a hundred million different components of national life to intelligibility but the notion of intelligibility itself.[28]

The interrogative mode of the *Forum* was a parody of dialogue. As such, it was calculated perfectly to convey easy assumptions and false certainties about an answerable world. Editorials and articles in the *Forum* invoked rhetorical positivism. When they ask "What constitutes a good poem?" or "How shall war be abolished?" the implication is not only that answers are simply a matter of means *but that questions are successful formulations of ideas.*[29] But there are wheels within wheels: questions were redirective. They were meant to establish intellectual (and even economic) parameters of inquiry. A recent history of American business in the twenties argues that questions about war and peace were intended to point toward particular answers. This book cites Thurman Arnold on the sources and aims of approved ideas: "Men began to dream of a new world order in which both panics and wars could be eliminated. Panics would be impossible because all industry was regulated by sound banking houses, which would come to the rescue when danger threatened. Wars would be impossible because international business, which had everything to lose and nothing to gain by war, would prevent any powerful and civilized nation from aggression."[30] This kind of thinking was a slick new version of the Idea of Progress, with failed systems of historical prediction replaced by other systems on their own way to failure.

One understands after reading *Babbitt* and *Middletown* that business ideology dominated the twenties. However, this is not entirely about businessmen in charge. The conception of arriving at knowledge through ques-

tion and answer had recently been undermined. The burden of philosophy, well understood by the mid-twenties, was that certain questions not
only have no answers—they cannot even be formulated.[31] Yet, questions
in the *Forum* were characteristically directed at the quick solution of im-
ponderables by technological means. The *Forum* prided itself on apply-
ing "technological habits of thinking" to things not scientific.[32] Here is
Hemingway's narrator musing over a particular statement: "Our deepest
convictions—will Science upset them?" (360).[33] The point of the editors is
that science can solve anything; his point is that the editors have no idea
what anyone's "deepest convictions" may be.

Walter Lippmann identified a central problem about convictions: our
"profusion of creeds and philosophies, fads and intellectual experiments"
may come to us from sources much satisfied with themselves—but these
ideas remain "accidental visions of the world."[34] Hemingway's own views
of systematic explanation, by contrast, are in the philosophical main-
stream. In one of the best-known essays of the twentieth century, Isaiah
Berlin's "The Hedgehog and the Fox," we see Tolstoy's reaction to those
"bogus solutions" offered up so plentifully by the apparatus of thought.
The presumption that all things are answerable, Berlin says, is "an insult to
the intelligence." There is one passage that the reader of *A Farewell to Arms*
can't afford to ignore: it praises twentieth-century existentialism, which rejected "all explanations as such because they are a mere drug to still serious
questions, shortlived palliatives for wounds which are unbearable but must
be borne, above all not denied or 'explained'; *for all explaining is explaining
away* [emphasis added], and that is a denial of the given—the existent—
the brute facts."[35] In "The Originality of Machiavelli" Berlin makes a sharp
distinction between predictive intellectual schemes and the resistant "human material" that they pretended to understand.[36] In "The Counter-
Enlightenment" he reminds intellectuals that there has been more than
one tradition of Western thought.[37] It might well be that inquiry and
questioning—which so easily decline into rationalism—don't proceed to
the heart of anything. Hemingway's opinions tend to be expressed in a
language of scorn and resentment that often implies the marginality of the
speaker. But the content of his opinions is by no means marginal.

The narrator of "Banal Story" cites and parodies the *Forum*: "Our children's children—what of them? Who of them? New means must be dis-

covered to find room for us under the sun. Shall this be done by war or can it be done by peaceful methods?" Or, "Our civilization—is it inferior to older orders of things?" (360–61). One notes that such questions are implicit in Hemingway's war novels. Implicit, but not answerable. Here, the tortuous movement from war to peace takes place in a single sentence. I note that it was written just after the age of Wilson and the (failed) League of Nations. The argument or rather echo of the argument on civilization reduces John Dewey and Walter Lippmann—and all other serious consideration of the subject—to midcult breathlessness. Most noticeably, the passage is an expansion of familiar tactics: a shower of questions delivered under the impression that the form is adequate to the substance. But the form fights the substance. The form is so trivial that the substance becomes parodic. Most interesting is that phenomenon noted by Lippmann in *A Preface to Morals,* the extraction of different concepts from incommensurable systems. In America, an idea comes from anywhere and has a lifetime one sentence long. It is derived—nothing like a rule, which imposes itself by its heavier experiential weight of being.

Hemingway was especially conscious of facile literary explanations.[38] Here is an actual passage from the *Forum* on the reading of writing: "Is it merely a matter of opinion, of individual taste?—Or are there standards which must be adhered to? By whom were they established?"[39] It is jarring, after the introduction of that phrase "opinion," to hear the fake equability of what follows. Is any "opinion" ever that open to discussion? More to the point, whose "opinion" matters? This kind of statement moves the discussion into Hemingway's own *querencia:* "He told George Plimpton in a *Paris Review* interview that 'Joyce was a very great writer and he would only explain what he was doing to jerks. Other writers that he respected were supposed to be able to know what he was doing by reading him'." In the same interview, Hemingway added that "It is very bad for a writer to talk about how he writes. He writes to be read by the eye and no explanations or dissertations should be necessary. You can be sure that there is much more there than will be read at any first reading."[40]

The destination of "Banal Story" is the death of the bullfighter Maera, a figure so important to Hemingway that he returned to him in "Chapter xiii," "Chapter xiv," "The Undefeated," and *Death in the Afternoon.*[41] Getting to that destination is difficult—we first have to run the gamut of remarks from the *Forum*, then navigate from satire to tragedy. And there is an impasse in the story because Hemingway does not provide us with a transition: first we are reading a magazine, and then we are suddenly at a deathbed. But there are connections: both "Banal Story" and "The Undefeated" are about Maera's death; both are about the failure of critics to understand it; and both distinguish between an experience undergone and its explanation. This part of the story has an intrusive new vocabulary of the body: until now we have read, selectively, about the mind. The flotilla of remarks from the *Forum* have reflected a view of life entirely orderly, rationalistic, understandable. That view depends on categorical abstractions like "Science" and "civilization." At no point has individual experience been touched. But the story ends with a tremendous existential description of Maera on his deathbed, in a dark room, choking his life out with a tube in each of his lungs, drowning as he tries to breathe. Maera dies painfully. He has his funeral. Men take his picture away with them, and life goes on. His suffering, as in Auden's "*Musée des Beaux Arts*," occurs while no one "sees" it.

In 1929, when the manuscript chapters of *A Farewell to Arms* were discussed by Max Perkins and Robert Bridges, another deathbed scene confronted middlebrow taste. Death and suffering at the novel's end were, it appeared, too graphic for critics, editors, and the national audience. Here is Max Perkins, telling Hemingway why truth and serialization did not go together for either of his novels of the twenties:

> You as an ex-newspaperman know about such things, and that there is a practical side to running periodicals.-On the other hand, there is this other side which I can not wholly overlook:-there was a great deal of hostility to "The Sun". It was routed and driven off the field by the book's qualities, and the adherence which they won. The hostility was very largely that which any new thing in art must meet, simply because it is disturbing. It shows life in a different aspect, and people are more comfortable when they have got it all conventionalized and smoothed down, and everything unpleasant hidden. Hostility also partly came from those who actually did not understand the book because its method of expression was a new one. . . . It was the same failure to be understood that a wholly new painter meets.

People simply do not understand because they can only understand what they are accustomed to.[42]

This did not put an end to the argument about the presence of death in Hemingway and the language he used to describe it. A few months later, Perkins said the following of *A Farewell to Arms:* "I know how people shrink from the truth, not only in life, but even more in literature,- and particularly those people beyond middle age who are not accustomed to it in their literature, certainly not in the pages of a magazine."[43]

The two halves of Hemingway's story do not meet. There are few conceivable questions (for example, shall we abandon bullfights? would better medical assistance have prevented this?) that might illuminate a hard life, or any life, and a brutal death. "Banal Story" is easy to under-value because of the roughly mitered joint between satire and tragedy. But Hemingway's impasse is intentional. He contrasts two halves of the story because his subject is fake ideas that resist bodily facts. It was an American issue: William James had in the previous generation observed that "idealism, thinking of reality only under intellectual forms, knows not what to do with *bodies* of any grade."[44] Like Santayana, another great observer of the American scene, James was thinking both of a philosophical mode and also of the character of our daily life.[45] Sentimental idealism—characteristic of our public life—wants answers, not questions. It wants facts to be absorbed and colored by values. Max Perkins seems to have described the American audience with great clarity: middle-class Americans in a censorious decade who valued decency over actuality. They were nervous about looking at the human body for evidence of ideas, so that the sickness and violence in Hemingway were as anxiety-provoking as sexuality. They did not want to know about Maera's deathbed or anything else to do with the body's mystery. Hemingway's version of the *Forum* was all mental reflex and physical revulsion. Its editorial object was "to interpret the New America That Is Attaining National Consciousness in the Decade in which We Live," and he simply allowed it, after its fashion, to succeed.

3
Fitzgerald
Time, Continuity, Relativity

George Santayana, in *Character and Opinion in the United States* (1920), recalls that "the President of Harvard College, seeing me once by chance soon after the beginning of a term, inquired how my classes were getting on; and when I replied that I thought they were getting on well, that my men seemed to be keen and intelligent, he stopped me as if I was about to waste his time. 'I meant,' said he, '*what is the number* of students in your classes'?"[1] Enough said, but there is a larger satirical target in view, the transformation of "respect for quantity" into our national philosophy. Santayana begins his essay on the materialist mind by asking the reader first to imagine "the great emptiness of America" because the filling-up of wilderness depends on measure if only for geographical location. Materialism works: we estimate whether we can get through a winter, how much land we can clear, what the profit will be. Later, even in the civilized condition, we measure what we have and how long it has taken to get where we are. Is this view persuasive? The evidence seems to support Santayana: in 1927, Charles A. and Mary R. Beard described the omnipresence of "size . . . quantity . . . avoirdupois . . . the yardstick. . . . mass, number, velocity" in the national imagination. They added that the acceleration of scientific research was making the pursuit of numerical detail the dominant model of intellectual operation. This was bound, they concluded, to affect artistic reasoning.[2]

In 1925, Fitzgerald, with his own eye on quantifying experience, wrote about the way a certain American might think about number and continuity:

> "My house looks well, doesn't it?" he demanded. "See how the whole front of it catches the light."
>
> I agreed that it was splendid.
>
> "Yes." His eyes went over it, every arched door and square tower. "It took me just three years to earn the money that bought it."[3]

When life's conditions are material so inevitably is their interpretation.[4] Yet Santayana and other writers understood that while materialism works, it also doesn't work. It can never fully correspond to reality, because much human experience is incommensurate. However, like Jay Gatsby, Americans never give up trying to impose quantity upon experience. Here is another Fitzgerald text that—characteristically—deals with the quantity of time:

> The Knickerbocker Bar, beamed upon by Maxfield Parrish's jovial, colorful "Old King Cole," was well crowded. Amory stopped in the entrance and looked at his wrist watch: he wanted particularly to know the time, for something in his mind that catalogued and classified like [sic] to chip things off cleanly. Later it would satisfy him in a vague way to be able to think: "That thing ended at exactly twenty minutes after eight on Thursday, June 10th, 1919." This was allowing for the walk from her house.[5]

Amory Blaine tends to be humorless—this is a comedy of national solipsism. However, even Amory seems aware that little in life is ever "exactly" settled, much less portal to portal. He realizes that the quantification of proof, which belongs to science, may be connected to will and possibly to obsession. He knows that nothing in life is less likely than containing experience in bundles of time. This was to be an intellectual topic of 1922, and more needs to be said of it. For now, we keep in mind the contradiction of classifying things that resist measure.

A great change in thinking about the self within time had come about early in Fitzgerald's life. One began by accepting "the uninterrupted forward movement of clocks, the procession of days, seasons, and years" as a way of thinking about historical time and also as a way of thinking about values.[6] Stating something chronologically explains it. It also translates it: "forward movement" became a metaphor of intellectual and even of moral advancement. That is one reason why the "future" is so important to American midcult thinking—it can so easily be confused with progress. Such conceptions were due for revaluation:

> This shift in attention from the historical past to the personal past was part of a broad effort to shake off the burden of history. By focusing on the immediate past of individuals . . . thinkers and artists sharpened the analyses of their philosophical studies . . . and intensified the dramatic impact of their literary works. The historical past was the source of social forces over which they had little control; it created institutions that had lasted for centuries; and it limited their sense of autonomy. The overbearing deterministic formal systems of nineteenth-century historicism produced broad, general laws of history, whereas these thinkers wanted to understand the unique responses of individuals to particular circumstances. . . . They did not want to imitate the art of the past, and they did not want their lives to be regulated by social conventions that were conceived in the distant past and over which they had no control. . . . They focused their attention on the personal past, because they believed it to be a richer source of subject matter than the remote and impersonal historical record.[7]

The new habit of mind would lead to intellectual independence. Yet, as a recent history of modernism puts it, there is no guarantee of truth from multiplied perspectives. An age of intellectual atomism will almost certainly be an age of discontinuity. The idea of personal truth can lead (as in the case of Jay Gatsby) to incommunicative "radical subjectivity."[8] Many of Fitzgerald's references to time imply both the need for continuity and its impossibility.

We think of how many references to time in the twenties insist on its linearity. Titles like *The Outline of History* by H. G. Wells or *The Rise of American Civilization* by the Beards have a time line built into them. The famous last chapter of Wells's book is titled "The Next Stage of History." Wells's book, a best-seller in both 1920 and 1921, foretells "the coming age" or the future designed by the present. That is in itself a definition of linearity. The book's great hope is for "change," but the argument for change is never about unspecified or even undesired change; it is about the conformity of then to now. The world, Wells says, "progresses and will progress," meaning that change and progress are both linear and identical.[9]

There was much investment in the idea of linear time. The phrase *progressive* connoted both improvement and the passage of time. The Beards identified the main theme of American life as idealized materialism: "belief in unlimited progress—the continuous fulfillment of the historic idea which had slowly risen through the eighteenth and nineteenth century to a position of commanding authority."[10] The critical vocabulary of a major presence like Van Wyck Brooks is built around phrases like *evolution* and *development* with their own dual implications. Lewis Mumford reflexively situates cultural solutions in "future" time.[11] In all cases a relationship between time and will is presupposed. But one essential variant of modernism was the relativity of time, a subject often on Fitzgerald's mind.

Throughout his early life the idea had been at least as prevalent as that of time's linearity. One of the great events of 1922, that signal year recognized by Fitzgerald, was Walter Lippmann's review in *Public Opinion* of the ways in which we were then thinking about time. The Lippmann essay was intended to summarize contemporary theory on time for a general intellectual audience. He noted especially that "a presumption about time enters widely into our opinions. To one person an institution which has existed for the whole of his conscious life is part of the permanent furniture of the universe: to another it is ephemeral. Geological time is very different from biological time. *Social time is most complex*."[12] Lippmann's development of the latter point may well have something to do with our interpretation of *The Great Gatsby:* "an important part of wisdom is the ability to distinguish the time-conception that properly belongs to the thing in hand. The person who uses the wrong time-conception ranges from the dreamer who ignores the present to the philistine who can see nothing else. A true scale of values has a very acute sense of relative time."[13] Without being reductive, we may be able to see in this tripartite contemporary theory the outlines of Jay Gatsby, Tom Buchanan, and Nick Carraway.

Before Lippmann, both Josiah Royce and William James had stated that any idea of a moment experienced had to be modified by the realization that it was by no means instantaneous. Instead, time has a "specious" nature, that is, it contains previous moments and is emotionally and intellectually extended by them. It was common even by the turn of century to believe that apprehension of the "now" embraced that of the past. Gertrude Stein had written of a "continuous present" that surrounded any given instant:

> Beginning again and again is a natural thing even where there is a series.
> Beginning again and again and again explaining composition and time is a natural thing.[14]

Perhaps the most important reference to this subject was Bertrand Russell's long analysis of language and memory in 1921. He believed it plainly evident that images of the past were contained in present experience. Memory was in fact a kind of "experience of succession," an idea that provides a context for Fitzgerald's ideas about the tenacious hold of the past on the present. It is important to note that word "images" used by Russell, because at the center of his theory is the axiom that memory takes the form of images that later "are accompanied by a feeling of belief." They can, in fact, retain their full and original power of sensation.[15]

During the 1920s then, grounds existed for believing that the nature of time had become significantly more complex. It was both linear and also something more than linear. Lippmann's summation reached a wide audience who were to become familiar with a "continuous" present, an "immediate" present, a "perceptual present," and an even larger "ideational present." He writes that, "through the combination of perceptions with memory images, entire days, months, and even years of the past are brought together into the present."[16] Remorselessly practical, however, Lippmann argues against the tendency of mind to exaggerate any component. Imagining the future is, he states, particularly "illusive." The act of imagining must infallibly be colored by hope or by doubt. There is then much to think of in regard to depicting acts within time and thoughts about time in the twenties. Desire and hope argue for linearity, but reality argues otherwise.

On the simplest level, Fitzgerald's practice was to locate his essays, reviews, letters, and fiction within a chronology.[17] He frames his own descriptions by the accurate measurement of elapsed time within his own life—the years from 1919–30 are especially thick with allusion. "Echoes of the Jazz Age" (1931) bounces back and forth in time in order to come up with a coherent sense of development. First in order are "the Yellow Nineties" (13) culminating in 1902, then the war, and then the "ten-year period" from "the time of the May Day riots in 1919" to the decade's "spectacular death in October, 1929" (13). After 1920, "people over twenty-five" (16) became aware that the past had disappeared. Each succeeding year of the decade brought some new awareness: of sexual mores in 1920, obscenity in 1921, of age and desire in 1922 (17). The essay keeps retracing its steps, proceeding in time from the old world of 1915 to the time when commandments broke down in 1917 to the "events of 1919" (14), which assume greater importance in Fitzgerald's mind than those of the preceding five years. There is finally—"May one offer in exhibit the year 1922!" (15)—the sense that number is a form of intelligibility.[18]

Chronology prevails in these kinds of references. The connection of time and event is a form of explanation. Most of these connections refer to the years of his own life. Fitzgerald refers as a matter of course to the past of living memory—his own living memory. It is an efficient way of projecting his own and national solipsism. Dates are the bookends for his experience, and between dates are quantities of time measuring self-awareness. In 1932 ("My Lost City") he writes about his "first symbol" of New York, then about the time "five years later when I was fifteen" when he made "the girl" of the movies his second symbol (23), then about a day in April when he spotted Edmund Wilson on a rainy street and incarnated him as the third and latest version of the "Metropolitan spirit" (24). Within numbers are more numbers, because as Fitzgerald sees these moments in time, they may be complex but are not relative. The year 1912 is when grandmothers threw away their crutches and took lessons in the tango (18). The year 1913 becomes inevitably part of 1921 when the actresses seen on the earlier date become guests at Fitzgerald's house—although by this time all three symbols of the city had lost their meaning (29). The year 1914 becomes absorbed into dreams that failed to make it to decade's end and is connected to his own coming irrelevance sometime, he guesses, around 1945 (33). The year 1915 is one of discovery by most people of the mobile privacy of the automobile (14). The year 1917 is when the subject was covered by the *Yale Record* and the *Princeton Tiger* (15). The year 1919 is much more serious altogether, a landmark of May Day riots, cynicism, sex, and unwilling entanglement in life (13, 14, 17, 25). The years of the early twenties become completely absorbed into, form part of the identity of the Fitzgeralds (42–47). But quantity and time exist independently beyond their relationship to ourselves. Here are Scott and Zelda ("Auction—Model 1934") on Lot 15, a collection of symbolic things: "We have five phonographs, including the pocket ones, and no radio, eleven beds and no bureau. We shall keep it all—the tangible remnant of the four hundred thousand we made from hard words and spent with easy ones these fifteen years" (62). The numbers, quite literally, don't add up.

Sequential time in Fitzgerald is referred to by the actual measurement of minutes, hours, days, seasons, and years, and also by its artifacts: in *The Great Gatsby* there is a railroad timetable of July 5, 1922, a SCHEDULE of September 12, 1906, a clock that falls from Gatsby's mantlepiece.[19] But chronology is not certainty. In "Dalyrimple Goes Wrong," a "time-clock" must be punched every morning at seven, which has different meanings for different observers. The time it calculates is not progressive: "Unpleasant facts came to his knowledge. There were 'cave-dwellers' in the basement who had worked there for ten or fifteen years at sixty dollars a month, rolling barrels and carrying boxes through damp, cement-walled corridors, lost in that echoing half-darkness between seven and five-thirty and, like himself, compelled several times a month to work until nine at night."[20] Immersed in number, we realize that it may have no relationship either to sequence or progress. A list of years in "His Russet Witch" may answer Daisy's question in *The Great Gatsby* about what we do with the second half of life: "The years between thirty-five and sixty-five revolve before the passive mind as one unexplained, confusing merry-go-round. . . . For most men and women these thirty years are taken up with a gradual withdrawal from life. . . . we sit waiting for death."[21] In "The Sensible Thing" time is measured by minutes; in "The Ice-Palace" and a number of other stories it is measured by generations. Fitzgerald uses generations to emphasize time's discontinuity.

Mrs. Buckner in "The Scandal Detectives" is a living hiatus of American history: she believes that her son's relationship to her is the same as her relationship to the past. But her thoughts are not comprehensible to him—although they might well have been to her own great-grandmother.[22] Time's discontinuity includes Mrs. Harvey of "Bernice Bobs Her Hair," who knows that "modern situations were too much for her."[23] History is in itself a discontinuous experience, or at least living through it is.

The idea is nowhere more poignantly stated than in Fitzgerald's 1933 tribute to Ring Lardner, who "went on seeing, and the sights traveled back to the optic nerve, but no longer to be thrown off in fiction, because they were no longer sights that could be weighed and valued by the old criteria" (36–7). This was not the first time that Fitzgerald used the conception: the scene at Myrtle Wilson's party in *The Great Gatsby* describes confusion and even "blind eyes" through the smoke. It antedates the metaphorical meanings of the Lardner elegy. But those meanings were part of the intellectual context: we see in a 1930 essay of John Dewey *that writers especially, with their connection to both past and present,* share "the unreality that has overtaken traditional codes." In a new, relativistic world, the metaphor of impaired sight was often used. Here is Dewey's version: "instances of the flux in which individuals are loosened from the ties that once gave order and support to their lives are glaring. They are indeed so glaring that they blind our eyes to the causes which produce them. Individuals are groping their way through situations. . . . The beliefs and ideals that are uppermost in their consciousness are not relevant to the society in which they outwardly act and which constantly reacts upon them. Their conscious ideas and standards are inherited from an age that has passed away; their minds . . . are at odds with actual conditions."[24] The metaphor of impaired sight provides a context for Fitzgerald's language within the reverberation of ideas in the twenties and thirties.[25]

Dewey's "traditional codes" seem identical to Fitzgerald's "old criteria," and he too seems to find special significance in the fault line between generations. A number of Fitzgerald's stories retain memories of "an age that has passed away." One thinks especially of Fitzgerald's southern stories:

"The Ice Palace" opens with the loss of time past—although the main point turns out to be the difficulty of entering time present. That is the difficulty of the Jelly-bean in all his incarnations. Outside the South, "At Your Age" suggests its own disconnection. The ostensible subject of "The Lost Decade" is being drunk for ten years together. I think, however, that that is a figurative way of imagining the mysterious present in which everything we know has to be relearned. The story is not about the difficulty of drying out (which might well have been its logical center) but rather about the difficulty of recognizing new codes of reality. Because of that, the story is less real but more thematic. "Three Hours Between Planes" concludes that the duty of the second half of life is to forget the first. This is less easy than it sounds, and the power of "Babylon Revisited" consists of its refutation of that possibility. "The Rich Boy" solves the problem of life by never entering the present. Anson Hunter keeps on repeating the past, and the cruise with which the story ends is in fact a kind of circle back to it. Braddock Washington in "The Diamond as Big as the Ritz" memorably asks God only for one simple thing, that time should always be as it was yesterday. Basil Duke Lee understands that if we cannot make the sun stand still, at least we can make him run: "Like most Americans, he was seldom able really to grasp the moment, to say: 'This, for me, is the great equation by which everything else will be measured; this is the golden time,' but for once the present was sufficient. He was going to spend two hours in a country where life ran at the pace he demanded of it."[26]

～

Relativity is a familiar subject in modernism—but it may not be a metaphor. There were good reasons for Lippmann to connect his essay on time with another essay on space. Between *The Outline of History* in 1920 and *Public Opinion* in 1922 had come Einstein's Nobel Prize in 1921. This brought Einstein's defining work of 1905 back to public awareness—especially the relativity of time and space. By 1922 it was getting easier to understand how Einstein had changed the Newtonian formulation. Or, at least, people were becoming more familiar notionally with that change: "Einstein . . . considered that his new physics had fused time and space—separate categories in Newton's world. . . . his conclusion, as he explained in 1916, was the same as that of the joy-riding Marinetti: 'the world in which we live is a four-dimensional space-time continuum.' He emphasized that this was a world in which we all lived, not some Platonic heaven thought up by physicists; the earth, as Gertrude Stein claimed, truly is different in the twentieth century. . . . His paper on relativity in 1905 disrupted forever the equability of Newton's duration."[27] The idea and also the mechanisms cited by Einstein—mechanical objects moving through space—were quickly taken up by modernists. Edward Steichen had already in 1920 photographed a scene called "Time-Space Continuum." Naum Gabo issued a manifesto in that year stating that "space and time are reborn to us today." André Breton stated in 1921 that "belief in an absolute time and space seems about to vanish."[28] The year 1922 began a signal period for modernists: Michael Reynolds writes that in March of that year, "while Hemingway was learning his way about Paris, Albert Einstein was in town delivering a series of lectures. Einstein, whose first theoretical paper on relativity was published in 1905, had, by 1925, become a world celebrity whose picture needed no caption. His name and his ideas were bandied about in the popular press as frequently as they appeared in scientific journals. Between 1922 and 1928 the *New York Times* carried 172 stories about Einstein; during the same period almost a hundred articles about Einstein appeared in English and American periodicals."[29] Einstein contributed a new imagery: mechanical objects moving at high speeds in literature share some of the meanings they had for science:

> To explain the theory of relativity you need to imagine what Einstein called an "inertial frame of reference"—that is, something three-dimensional moving steadily. Actually you need at least two of these, because "moving" is not something one can do alone. To get them "moving" you need them to have different speeds or directions, because of the basic "principle of relativity" that nothing moves in any sense unless there is something else against which you can measure its motion. . . . What actual things Einstein had in mind when he came up with the theory that May we do not know—perhaps bicycles; but when he wrote a book to explain it to lay people in 1916, he used a railroad car moving past an embankment. To get the most startling results, the movement of the frames of reference with

respect to each other should be very fast; by 1925, Russell's colleague Alfred North Whitehead was using automobiles. Now we tend to use spaceships."[30]

One of the central figures in a great dialogue about space, time, and literature was Edmund Wilson, who in 1927 reviewed the problem of "making the universe seem somewhat less fantastic than, on Einstein's view, it must appear."[31] He thought that Einstein's new physics had made insuperable difficulties for the novelistic portrayal of conventional reality. Because of that, Wilson was ready to believe in the philosophy of Alfred North Whitehead, which was altogether more comforting. Whitehead, among other things, was skeptical of the theory of relativity. He offered his own way of understanding objects located in time. However, by 1931, Wilson had made his peace with relativity—he now considered it to be a norm—and he was able to write this of Proust's application, conscious or not, of Einstein:

> For Proust, though all his observations seem relative, does, like Einstein, build an absolute structure for his world of appearances. His characters may change from bad to good, from beautiful to ugly, as Einstein's measuring-rods shrink and elongate, his clocks become accelerated or retarded; yet as Einstein's mathematical apparatus enables us to establish certain relations between the different parts of the universe, in spite of the fact that we do not know how the heavenly bodies are moving in respect to one another and no matter from what point of view our measurements have been made—so Proust constructs a moral scheme out of phenomena whose moral values are always shifting.[32]

Axel's Castle concludes with a set of observations on the contemporary understanding of science, chief among them that modernist literature "is evidently working, like modern scientific theory, toward a totally new conception of reality." Specifically, when we write according to the tenets of symbolism, we are in fact writing in the new "technical language of science." Finally, according to Wilson, one accomplishment of modernist writers has been to have "succeeded in effecting in literature a revolution analogous to that which has taken place in science and philosophy."[33]

We expect Fitzgerald, like those others on Wilson's mind, to have stated experience according to contemporary theories about it. The surmise is tested by Fitzgerald's description of time experienced while moving through space:

> After a while the porter closed the vestibule door and passed back along the corridor, and we slid out of the murky yellow station light and into the long darkness. What I remember next must have extended over a space of five or six hours, though it comes back to me as something without any existence in time—something that might have taken five minutes or a year.[34]

As a recent history of science points out, time had become relative: "When we say, 'Something happened *at the moment* I was talking on the phone,' we imply that there is some universal *moment* to be *at.* . . . But just as Einstein's special theory derailed the moving train of sequence, it also detonated the station house of simultaneity. The idea of a static moment that contains events concurrent with one another blew to scattered bits because, according to Einstein's equations, each exploding piece of debris existed in its own inertial frame of reference with its own time and space *relative* to every other reference frame each containing its own special time and space."[35] In the Fitzgerald passage, quantifying time does the opposite of locating us in the world of realism. The combination of time and space has been linked to the combination of train and station—all of which derive from Einstein's illustration of the theory of relativity. Einstein had used the example of a train leaving its station to show that, at different speeds, observers would at different points have different understandings of the same thing.

A car in the twenties was a commodity, a conveyance, and a status symbol. It was also an object moving through space while redefining one's previous understanding of time. Cars, trains, and planes had double lives as referents. A year after the publication of Fitzgerald's novel, Alfred North Whitehead wrote that "in the past human life was lived in a bullock cart; in the future it will be lived in an aeroplane; and the change of speed amounts to a difference in quality."[36] There is Gatsby's car in particular, which "sped along a cobbled slum lined with the dark, undeserted saloons of the faded gilt nineteen-hundreds" as he and Nick scatter light through half Astoria.[37] The association of space-speed-time is characteristic of Fitzgerald's images, as is the compressed view from the standpoint of the present. We are constantly reminded that the perspective of the viewer interprets the object perceived. One section of Fitzgerald's "Note-Books" describes the perfect solipsism of a couple who "rode through those five years in an open car with the sun on their foreheads and their hair flying" (146). In another section, a car drives "past the low Corinthian lines of the Christian Science Temple, past a block of dark frame horrors, a deserted row of grim red brick—an unfortunate experiment of the late 90's—then new houses again, bright blinding flowery lawns. These swept by, faded past, enjoying their moment of grandeur, then waiting there in the moonlight to be outmoded as had the frame, cupolaed mansions of lower down and the brownstone piles of older Crest Avenue in their turn" (227). It is an economical way of describing the illusion of permanence. But the larger meaning is that speed relativizes time. History is itself "waiting . . . to be outmoded," and the momentary view we get of it is metaphysically appropriate. There is no conventional way of stating the relationship of a historical artifact to the thirty seconds or so it takes to describe it, or to the five seconds or so it takes to drive by it.

Fitzgerald invokes time and space together, and often he will describe abruptly the presence of large-scale space in portrayals of limited space. Here is another passage that uses the railway car and station or embankment as they are used by Einstein:

He left feeling that if he had searched harder he might have found her—that he was leaving her behind. The day-coach—he was penniless now—was hot. He went out to the open vestibule and sat down on a folding chair, and the station slid away and the backs of unfamiliar buildings moved by. Then out into the spring fields, where a yellow trolley raced them for a minute with people in it who might once have seen the pale magic of her face along the casual street.

The track curved and now it was going away from the sun which, as it sank lower, seemed to spread itself in benediction over the vanishing city where she had drawn her breath. He stretched out his hand desperately as if to snatch only a wisp of air, to save a fragment of the spot that she had made lovely for him. But it was all going by too fast now for his blurred eyes. . . . [38]

Fitzgerald introduces more than one kind of space to intensify our sense of relativity—in fact, place becomes space. We are made to feel the earth itself sliding away from our consciousness of it, a situation addressed more than once in this novel. Fitzgerald invokes cosmic movement for more than romantic purposes: it allows him to imply the passage of more than one kind of time. And something familiar is made relative in time as it moves. We lose the capacity to quantify, although time is itself quantity. The astonishing expansion of this scene is itself momentary. As soon as the passage ends, it is enfolded in a scheme of time that appears to be familiar and sequential: the first phrase we hear next is that it is nine o'clock in the morning; then, that this day is different from yesterday; then that the pool is going to be drained today; that leaves will soon start to fall; that Gatsby doesn't want the pool done today; that he hasn't used it all summer; that it is twelve minutes before Nick's train leaves for New York. Nick will call about noon as promised, and he takes a later train home, but Gatsby will be dead by then. The scheme is a paradigm of a new form of actuality. Fitzgerald alternates objective and subjective understanding.

More important, our understanding of the *idea* of the present changes. Nick guesses that Gatsby came to see an "unfamiliar" world just before he died: as he looked around his pool, suddenly even common things took on frightening and grotesque shapes in "a new world, material without being real."[39] The cited phrases are more elegant than the language of contemporary science but convey the same message: in 1921, A. S. Eddington had explained the new physics in a book aimed at laymen. In this book, he connected the idea of a new world to examples chosen from works of literature. Eddington described relativity as a correction to the sight of our "two eyes." We needed a new interpretation of the way things really were because it was mere custom that persuaded us to see what we thought our eyes saw. That would help us get a new and more accurate "picture of the world."[40] The new picture should displace what Fitzgerald was soon to describe as "the old warm world" of our imagination. Eddington argued that everything perceived needed to be relativized, or understood as having more than one relationship to the viewer's mind. He cited what he called the principle of reciprocity of size in Swift, which meant seeing life first as a giant, later as a dwarf in order to understand that at different times perceptions were different—and also true in their difference. Eddington thought that different-but-true perceptions were native to science and "a necessary consequence of the Principle of Relativity."[41] The way to understand relativity—and modernity—was, he said, to read *Gulliver's Travels* and also *Alice in Wonderland.*[42]

We all believe in Occam's razor, and it does no good to multiply probabilities. The instinctive conclusion may well be that Fitzgerald uses hundreds of units of time because they are common signifiers of realism. He places them throughout his writing to provide a sense of quantifiable fact. But that does not take into account the alternation of relative and sequential time in that writing, especially those differences in conceptions of time noted by Lippmann in 1922. It ignores the debate on time from 1905 through 1922. It fails to take account of what Whitehead in 1925 called the "effects on social life arising from the new situation." He did not mean by this that intellectuals necessarily understood the new laws of physics: "we are not concerned with details, but with ultimate influences on thought."[43] So it is not a good choice to believe that Fitzgerald uses time to put up signposts of reality in the form of realism. When he addresses time he links it not only to space but to our subjective understanding. In short, he refers to relativity as the issue had been refracted over his lifetime. Since the issue was still being mentally adjudicated, there was more than one way to think about it: "Novelty, as empirically found, doesn't arrive by jumps and jolts, it leaks in insensibly, for adjacents in experience are always interfused, the smallest real datum being both a coming and a going, *and even numerical distinctions* being realized effectively only after a concrete interval has passed." What finally happens is that "all the old identities at last give out."[44]

Joseph Conrad's insertion of geological time into narrative time in *Heart of Darkness* had become familiar, but Fitzgerald adds intimations of cosmic time, social time, and ideational time. He depicts the relative present. Certain stories—for example, "The Ice Palace"—create a moment intelligible only when developed from or differentiated from other measurable moments. We have to know about the Civil War, its casualties, its beliefs, its protagonists, its adversaries, and the generational sequence after it. We are made to sense time's imbalance. We have to see the way that time slowly unfolds in Tarleton, Georgia, as opposed to the way it speeds up in the North. It matters that Sally Carrol Happer has both a real and an imagined past—and that her northern admirer has neither. He consciously rejects such useless things, while her character is nothing less than composed of them. Throughout the fiction—and certainly the essays, letters, and reviews—Fitzgerald juxtaposes such differing conceptions of time. We think of Gatsby's clock, telling time (but not the right time) while it falls through space. All three people watching it have a different understanding of the present moment—and we begin to understand that time is "relative" in more than one way.[45]

4
Hemingway and the Authority of Thought

In life and literature Hemingway moved north-south and west-east, following the line Illinois-Italy-Paris-Spain-Key West-Africa-Cuba. There were epicycles within the orbit, and the pattern recurved. But there was a pattern, beginning with the departure from the United States and what it stood for, then toward the great European "centres of culture and civilization," and then to those places opposed to them.[1] The pattern was more than geographic, involving profound change in his religion, his ideas, and his subject. Regarding the last, Hemingway came to resemble Kipling and also experienced his fate. Critics expected literature to examine civilized life. Instead, these two writers changed intellectual geography. Henry James famously "deplored his friend's descent from 'the simple in subject to the more simple—from the Anglo-Indians to the natives, from the natives to the Tommies, from the Tommies to the quadrupeds, from the quadrupeds to the fish, and from the fish to the engines and screws'."[2] James thought that this indicated a choice between intellectual values and their opposites, which was partly true. But when Hemingway went from men to beasts to the fish of the sea a simpler subject did not imply a simpler set of ideas, although the critics thought even less of him for it than James did of Kipling.[3] After all, "What are bulls? Animals. Brute Animals" (197).

The values of complex thought asserted by James lost authority by the time they reached Hemingway because they were based on assumptions about what it was possible to know. Hemingway was particularly conscious of the difficulty of knowing—the phrases "talk" and "thought" in his writing are adversarial, deployed against their common usage. Against them are those other modalities of silence, questioning, deflection, skepticism. Ideas about thought, memory, perception, and experience changed definitively in the early twenties. Wittgenstein particularly provided a new conceptual vocabulary.

The idea of inquiry took on new meanings. Before the early twenties one naturally assigned to schematic thought the definition of social laws and of the good life. But Wittgenstein and others recognized insuperable obstacles to categorizing—or even understanding—human life. Throughout Wittgenstein's work one is confronted by a productive sense of difficulty. He understands how hard it is to make *any* kind of judgment about other minds. He continually reminds his interlocutors that their sense of otherness is based on assumptions because it is impossible to share, duplicate, or possibly understand experience. He argues for the description of life rather than the elucidation of answers for its problems. He concentrates on the use of precise language to define those problems that may, in some cases, be clarified. He is deeply skeptical of explanatory patterns imposed on our experience. Marjorie Perloff calls attention to some basic tenets, one being that "in philosophy there are no deductions: *it* is purely descriptive." The second states that "even if *all possible* scientific questions be answered, the problems of life have still not been touched at all."[4] Wittgenstein's ideas, then, premise a kind of separateness. It is hard to know one's self, harder to understand others, impossible to understand the relationship of all selves. In other words, the circumstances are ideal for reading Hemingway.

The subtitle of James Mellow's biography of Hemingway, *A Life without Consequences*, comes from "Soldier's Home." Mellow applied the phrase to Hemingway's distancing himself from others, especially from women. In the story, the context is the connection of thought to sexual love: "You did not need a girl unless you thought about them. He learned that in the army. . . . You did not have to think about it." The phrase about consequences connects also to "all this talking" that precedes sexual contact— and, conclusively, to the idea that "you did not need to talk."[5] The subject is less engrossing than the mode, sex taking up less intellectual space than the discussion of reasoning about it. The issue is not that one doesn't need women, but that one doesn't need thought. Is that because thought isn't needed in real life? Or because it leads to wrong conclusions? Because language is insufficient for thought? Because thought gives us the illusion of relationship to an object? What we take at first glance to be anti-intellectualism turns out to be more complex.[6]

In "The Undefeated" a specific problem about thought is posed. It functions, necessarily, through language. However, language is insufficient:

> He thought in bull-fight terms. Sometimes he had a thought and the particular piece of slang would not come into his mind and he could not realize the thought. His instincts and his knowledge worked automatically, and his brain worked slowly and in words. He knew all about bulls. He did not have to think about them. He just did the right thing. His eyes noted things and his body performed the necessary measures without thought. If he thought about it, he would be gone.[7]

The passage distinguishes between habit and instinct. It suggests how knowledge is accumulated and also how language translates ideas. It has a reasonably sophisticated sense of the problem of translation from mind to body. In fact, its thesis would have been reasonably familiar to the contemporary reader. Here is Bertrand Russell's 1921 conclusion on the mind-body connection: "Prejudice leads us to suppose that between the sensory stimulus and the utterance of the words a process of thought must have intervened, but there seems no good reason for such a supposition. Any habitual action, such as eating or dressing, may be performed on the appropriate occasion, without any need of thought, and the same seems to be true of a painfully large proportion of our talk. What applies to uttered speech applies of course equally to the internal speech which is not uttered. I remain, therefore, entirely unconvinced that there is any such phenomenon as thinking which consists neither of images nor of words, or that "ideas" have to be added to sensations and images as part of the material of which mental phenomena are built."[8] Russell was convinced that humans, like animals, reacted to "a certain sensory situation" in a predictable way. He stated that certain animals (dogs, cats, horses, and bears) reacted as any sentient being might to sensory information. We might certainly learn from them, and not as parables.

Who, in fact, do we learn from? A recent study of Wittgenstein states that "since the time of the Greeks the commonly accepted view draws a contrast between the philosopher and the ordinary person. It is the latter who is not reflective, who lives the unexamined life, who blindly follows conventions and authority (especially political authority), who lives in the world of appearance. . . . It is the philosopher who . . . discovers the true nature of things. . . . But Wittgenstein's originality consists in turning this picture on its head. It is the plain man who is all right, who is not troubled by mental cramps, and who does not cast up a dust that prevents him from seeing things as they are."[9] If this is true, then Hemingway's waiters, bullfighters, soldiers, ambulance attendants, hotel-owners, hunters, and smugglers have a certain authority. After all, seeing things as they are is nothing if not Socratic. Are Hemingway's figures know-nothings or skeptics? Are they empiricists? Radical empiricists? The odds are better on those things, I would guess, than on the surmise that they find knowledge useless. They may be rejecting not thought but its supposed connection to action and the larger relationship of thought to the discernment of truth. They may even echo Edmund Wilson, who thought a great deal about thought from the mid-twenties to the early thirties.

Wilson was concerned with two issues: the disconnection of thought from purpose and the impossibility of ascribing thought to literary characters. In 1924, reviewing the work of Gilbert Seldes, Wilson stated that the "inconsecutive" and "pointless" comedy featured in vaudeville was in actuality a counterpart to the worldview of Dada. Such a view mattered greatly, because it corresponded to the condition of the real world: "in France, the collapse of Europe and the intellectual chaos that accompanied it; in America—what is perhaps another aspect of a general crisis: the bewildering confusion of the modern city and the enfeeblement of the faculty of attention." His most important point was, I think, that such vaudeville scripts—the new comedy as a whole, contradictory, ironic, and resentful—showed us how our "own minds are beginning to work."[10] In a 1927 review of Alfred North Whitehead, Wilson wrote that Einstein's relativity theory had made it almost impossible to depict reality as it was now conceived.[11] In a letter of 1928 Wilson wrote of fiction at decade's end in which it is characteristic that "thoughts never pass into action."[12] In his journals Wilson noted that thought and feeling usually turned out to be "nonthinking and nonfeeling." The mind pretended to solve problems and tasks as it canvassed memories and images—but, because full consciousness was immensely difficult to attain, the process of thought was unproductive. Literature was, he said, especially affected by the failure of the author to "realize" the experience of his characters. Authorial thought was no more than an argument stating "that life is really like that for the author and is therefore capable of being made so for others."[13] In *Axel's Castle* (1931) Wilson singled out Paul Valéry's insight into "mind," which "turns out to have constructed its own universe." Symbolism demonstrates that our "habit of thinking"—even to the most basic conceptions of cause and effect—has been an intellectual imposition.[14]

Wilson's observations are contextual for "The Killers" and *The Sun Also Rises*. Both of these works of the mid-twenties refer to the process, value, and ends of thinking. Both have important skeptical dialogues about thought. In fact, both reserve their last lines for the subject. The former ends with practical advice about situations impossible to understand: "you better not think about it." The latter ends by reminding us ("Isn't it pretty to think so?") that fact is not the same as idea.

~

Wittgenstein asked in *Philosophical Investigations* "what is *thinking*?" and gave enough answers to keep writers busy for a generation. We might, he said, be thinking about something even if we were wrong about it; we might not even have meanings in mind because the language itself was the thought; and, most notably, we might never be sure that a given statement "is the correct translation of your wordless thought into words."[15] "Soldier's Home" certainly illustrates the difficulty of translating thought into words—and also the difficulty of understanding a given statement. Krebs's mother wants to know if her dear boy loves her. But that is impossible to answer because he doesn't love anyone.[16] When Krebs answers his mother's question with the word "No" he means two things: what he says is true, and he is unwilling to make any simple statement fit a complex reality. This goes along with his unwillingness to say anything about his war experience. In neither case can language be true to the immensely difficult task of translating either fact or feeling. When he says "I don't love anybody" there are psychological echoes. Before the war, Freud had formulated a nearly identical phrase, "*I do not love anyone*" and suggested a number of interpretations. Chief among them: "I love only myself." Other possibilities: megalomania—or possibly the consequence of having to choose between social demands and the urgent defense of the self's integrity.[17] After the war, Wittgenstein wrote that language disguises thought, that there is a huge difference between feeling something and expressing it— there may not be any emotive truth of the kind this passage demands.[18] In Hemingway, it is not easy to state feeling at any time. When a writer in the twenties takes up that particular issue—or invokes the opposition between telling and seeing—he makes an allusion.

"The Killers" is about a sequence of actions; its dialogues are largely about the assumptions of thought. One important subject is the difference between fact and interpretation. Thinking within a given structure—in this case, morality—prevents the recognition of meanings in events.[19] Max and Al have a lot to say about their line of work, about movies, vaudeville, and comedy. They also have much to say about the way things actually are. Where do George and Nick get their ideas about the coherence and intelligibility of life? From American idealism, which regards the world and the people in it as malleable substance. Does that idealism have anything to do with reality? William James and John Dewey had already warned Hemingway's audience that we saw the world not as it was, but as we wanted it to be. H. L. Mencken had recently identified idealism as a national superstition. He put the matter as plainly as it could be stated: Americans believed "that right and wrong are immovable things—that they have an actual and unchangeable existence."[20] Max and Al disprove that particular thought. The reiterations of their dialogue—which call forth responses from George and Nick, shaping the nature of their own language—provide a different set of inferences.

George and Nick may be said to think about thinking. They refer themselves to a structure of beliefs in place. They apply ideas about intelligibility and order not worked out by themselves, and they allow themselves to imagine that moral imperatives exist independently of the will to conceive them. When Max and Al talk about thinking they mean something very different. First, they are not much concerned with ends, which is to say, with the meaning of acts. They are concerned only with acts themselves, which is why there is no "idea" about anything. Second, they understand that the word "think" is as illusory as the word "know." In the early thirties, Hemingway used this locution to advise novelists about the relationship of the former to the latter: "Don't just think. . . . understand."[21] Thought may be the statement of received opinion. Understanding, which is empirical, concerns the thing at hand.

Thought in Hemingway is not consciousness itself, but it dominates consciousness. It can be involuntary, and it will certainly not be accurate. "Now I Lay Me" describes first the rejection of thought and then its avoidance.[22] I don't think these things become intelligible as exorcisms of trauma or as rituals. They pointedly depict the operation of mind. Thought (as Harry Morgan understands it in *To Have and Have Not*) not only obstructs action but misconstrues reality. Nick understands that it is better to rely on memory and perception than on ideas and explanations. It is difficult if not impossible to detach these things from thought. But Hemingway took this step because it allowed him to reject unconvincing explanation. What we call *thought* is in Hemingway the useless residue of culture.

In *The Sun Also Rises*, Robert Cohn and Jake Barnes have a long dialogue early on about going either to South America or British East Africa. Cohn insists that South America has captured his imagination, but Barnes recognizes the source of his argument, a novel by W. H. Hudson that "recounts splendid imaginary amorous adventures of a perfect English gentleman in an intensely romantic land, the scenery of which is very well described." The operative phrases are "imaginary," "gentleman," and "romantic." Cohn is not a gentleman, his South America does not exist, the world is not a romantic place. That much is visible from the statement and tone. But the argument, characteristic in Hemingway, is in a larger sense between derived thought and actual experience. Where do thoughts come from? Cohn turns down Africa because he has "never read a book about it" (9–10). In *A Farewell to Arms*, Frederic Henry is listening to his ambulance crew argue about ending the war. They are for unilateral disarmament, something between an idea and a dream. Henry's counterargument is grounded on probability: the war must be finished, not abandoned. In any case, leaving the field would only confirm victory for the opposition—and the Germans are unlikely to respond in kind. Men without guns can defend nothing. Passini—a victim of mass literacy—says this of his opinion: "We think. We read. We are not peasants."[23] It sounds virtuous, idealistic, and even wise. But the first two phrases are in fact identical: *what Passini thinks is what he has read.* One doesn't want to be paradoxical, but he has read and therefore he thinks that he thinks. There are few better examples in Hemingway of thought as derivation. As to that, Bertrand Russell was quite clear in 1921: "the reference of thoughts to objects. . . . seems to me to be derivative, and to consist largely in *beliefs:* beliefs that what constitutes the thought is connected with various other elements which together make up the object. You have, say, an image of St. Paul's, or merely the word 'St. Paul's' in your head. You believe, however vaguely and dimly, that this is connected with what you would see if you went to St. Paul's, or what you would feel if you touched its walls; it is further connected with what other people see and feel. . . . "[24]

Death in the Afternoon—more intellectually important than the criticism generated around it—is a precondition for understanding *The Sun Also Rises.* The first chapter of *Death in the Afternoon,* consistent with Hemingway's practice, argues that thought is generally derived from reading—which may account for his lifelong contempt for critics, even those who now and then praised him. What is generally called *thought* may be intellectual acquiescence:

At the first bullfight I ever went to I expected to be horrified and perhaps sickened by what I had been told would happen to the horses. Everything I had read about the bull ring insisted on that point; most people who wrote of it condemned bullfighting outright as a stupid brutal business, but even those that spoke well of it as an exhibition of skill and as a spectacle deplored the use of the horses and were apologetic about the whole thing. . . . I remember saying that I did not like the bullfights because of the poor horses. I was trying to write then, and I found the greatest difficulty, aside from knowing truly what you really felt, rather than what you were supposed to feel, and had been taught to feel, was to put down what

really happened in action; what the actual things were which produced the emotion that you experienced.[25]

The verbs "supposed" and "taught" imply dissociation, if not interference between fact and thought. The passage is illuminated when seen
against an idea developed by Donald Davidson: while a person will have a
thought unique to his own mind, "not only can others often learn what
we think . . . but the very possibility of thought demands shared standards
of truth and objectivity."[26] Our sense of the above passage and one that
corresponds to it in *The Sun Also Rises* will benefit from some comparisons.
The first is the relationship of Hemingway's explanation to that of Jake
Barnes: "I sat beside Brett and explained to Brett what it was all about. I
told her about watching the bull, not the horse, when the bulls charged the
picadors, and got her to watching the picador place the point of his pic so
that she saw what it was all about" (167). As for the second, the phrase
"explained . . . what it was all about" has certain echoes. Phrases have a life
of their own in Hemingway's works, resurfacing as he needs to reconsider
them. In "The Killers," written just before the novel, to know "what's it all
about?" is to move from ignorance to knowledge. But, far more important,
it means moving from one intellectual world to another by virtue of wit-
nessing and then recognizing reality. I don't think that Hemingway repeats
himself without purpose, and this brief burst of language with that phrase
twice repeated implies that it is possible to think about meaning—if real
thought is involved.

The third comparison is of special interest. Hemingway worked out his
ideas about the interference of derived thought with fact at the same time
that Wittgenstein was using the same vocabulary for the same purpose:

His remark in *Philosophical Investigations* (66), "Don't think, but
look!" expresses this idea in a compact form. There are several variations on it. . . . "In order to see more clearly, here as in countless similar cases, we must focus on the details of what goes on; must look at
them *from close to*" (50). The contrast between thinking and looking
closely is even carried over to his final notebook, *On Certainty*. . . .
All the distinctive doctrines of the later philosophy flow from the idea
Don't think, but look![27]

Hemingway calls this process "watching" and "seeing." He uses the phrase "what really happened"—Wittgenstein states the importance of "what goes on." He concludes that understanding consists of "seeing connexions."[28]

During the bullfight, Jake and Brett are involved in a process of watching and seeing. These provide the basis for understanding: "I had her watch how Romero took the bull away from a fallen horse. . . . She saw how Romero avoided every brusque movement. . . . She saw how close Romero always worked to the bull. . . . She saw why she liked Romero's cape-work and why she did not like the others" (167). There has been the same visual emphasis before the bullfight begins and also the same use of language: Brett says that she "couldn't help looking" at the horses; her remark is followed by Mike's "She couldn't take her eyes off them" (165). Is she involuntarily drawn toward blood on the sand? Nothing else in the text suggests that. A better interpretation is that her eyes have been opened. The matter concerns only technique: *Death in the Afternoon* states that "the rôle of the horse. . . . is an incident rather than an end." The horse is not there to be killed but simply to be a platform for "supporting the man who receives the charge and places his pic in such a manner as to force the bull to tire" before it can be worked by the matador.[29]

When Jake Barnes comments on the textual sources of Robert Cohn's ideas he implies more than lamentable romantic taste. In regard to the bullfight, "The Undefeated" informs us that there are several ways to understand reality. One is to deduce meaning from action, like the men of the *cuadrilla*. Speed, directional tendency, and maneuver are information developed from observation. The other, unfortunately, is exemplified by the substitute bullfight critic of *El Heraldo* who decides to leave because "if he missed anything he would get it out of the morning papers."[30] When we see this attitude in fiction we tend not to give it full attention. But the failure to "see" is insistently connected to the failure to think. The false text is always in the perspective, posing "as a guide-book to what life holds" (9).

An important vein of scholarship informs us that events in Hemingway are visually reported. Early on, Carlos Baker listed notes from Hemingway's *Paris 1922* manuscript, beginning with declarative phrases that emphasize the authority of seeing and watching—hence faithfully recording— a series of acts.[31] The Baker passage has been invoked to put a point on the argument that "seeing" effectively means accurate witness and is a kind of photographic technique.[32] Most recently and with greater acuity Scott Donaldson has written of the complexity of sight in a writer who became, "as Saul Bellow has said of the successful novelist, 'a world-class noticer.' As he grew older the emphasis shifted from grasshoppers and trout to the human beings he knew and felt strongly about. He looked at them as closely as he could. *He looked too, at what they were looking at, or away from.*"[33]

"The Undefeated" states that Manuel's eyes see "without thought."[34] We learn more about this from the study of perception. In *The Sun Also Rises,* Brett is a breathing character—but she is also a textbook case of empirical understanding. Certain passages in Wittgenstein argue that we solve problems not by getting new information but by the rearrangement of what is already known. In other words, a kind of readiness is involved in the character of mind. When Wittgenstein speaks of appropriate language he uses phrases such as commanding "*a clear view*" and getting a "perspicuous representation" of our object. Avrum Stroll summarizes the issue: in both the *Tractatus* and *Philosophical Investigations* "Wittgenstein is saying that the new method will allow a person to see the world as it really is. The notion of *seeing* is crucial in both texts."[35] The above covers Wittgenstein from the early twenties to the beginning of the next decade. My argument is by no means that Ernest Hemingway was a disciple of Ludwig Wittgenstein. It is, however, that no one concerned with the problems of perception, experience, and statement in that period could have avoided Wittgenstein. There is simply too much for coincidence. The new philosophy was focused "on the details of what goes on," that is, a variant of "something that was going on with a definite end."[36]

Sometimes, as in the corrida scenes of *The Sun Also Rises,* answers are provided to those many questions about what is going on. Hemingway's narrator, protagonists, or readers aren't likely to get to "know what it was about."[37] The issue recurs in Hemingway because it recurs throughout the philosophy of experience of his time. Here is John Dewey's summation on the connection of thought to fact:

> Thinking is thus equivalent to an explicit rendering of the intelligent element in our experience. . . . All that the wisest man can do is to observe what is going on more widely and more minutely and then

select more carefully from what is noted just those factors which point to something to happen. The opposites, once more, to thoughtful action are routine and capricious behavior. The former accepts what has been customary as a full measure of possibility and omits to take into account the connections of the particular things done.[38]

We keep in mind Hemingway's statement at the beginning of *Death in the Afternoon* about moving from coverage of war to coverage of the corrida. Both kinds of observation have to do with knowledge. Both allow the writer to know "what really happened in action"—and also "what the actual things were" that produced emotion. We infer that war was for Hemingway a kind of laboratory in which responses were accelerated and that it might take years of civilian life to produce the sequence of act and reaction that he needed to witness. The Great War (and the lesser wars after it that Hemingway had in mind) turned out to have useful exemplary meaning for perception. The Dewey essay that I have cited, as if driven by the reasoning later adduced by Hemingway, connects the suspicion of things that "fill our heads . . . like a scrapbook" to the experience of war.[39] In fact Dewey's essay has a fictional protagonist, a general who needs to understand the nature of reality on the battlefield. The battlefield illustrates important problems of cognition. For example, it provides that highly compressed chronology that is needed to make decisions intelligible. Dewey's point is the necessary failure of ordinary thought when overwhelmed by events. The specific problem is that the general has to make certain decisions. In order to do that, he must first assign meaning to "the bare facts of the given situation."[40] He needs analysis, testing, and corroboration, but he gets only inference and implication. He cannot see beyond his individual horizon, while the information reaching him has been diluted and is hypothetical. In short, the process of "actively thinking" assigns "meaning" to "data" while very much on one's own.[41] There is no help from outside, and Dewey's concern with "the particular things" perceived helps us to understand Hemingway's phrase "what the actual things were." In Dewey, war shows us the degree to which supposedly objective thought is itself unreliable, that we can never rely on thought that comes from outside the situation, and, finally, that thought is not a conclusion about any experience but rather a way of reaching a conclusion. The examples cited by

Dewey and also the questions provoked by them suggest the depiction of reality in the writing of fiction.

At first Hemingway appears to be impatient with the process of thinking; he even seems to be anti-intellectual. But while Hemingway rejects thinking, he does not reject thought. He put the matter this way in a letter to Archibald MacLeish: "Papa never could think good with his head but by Jesus he thinks good with his bones."[42] The point tends to be elided by the mode—but there is a point. It concerns what Dewey called that "which is going on." The idea of productive thought for John Dewey (and also for Jake Barnes) proceeds from "observation."[43] It is a response to fact. It may not have any connection to the knowledge that we bring to any encounter. To use Bertrand Russell's tough-minded phrase, it will differ from what "other people see or feel." It is, as one dialogue of *A Farewell to Arms* states, a matter of discovery: "I never think and yet when I begin to talk I say the things I have found out in my mind without thinking."[44]

5
Recurrence in Hemingway and Cézanne

Words and also forms in Hemingway have second lives, especially those motifs deriving from visual art. Necessarily, scholarly focus has been on Cézanne, who according to Hemingway himself was deeply influential. For Hemingway, the main issue was Cézanne's ability to interpret landscape—not with documentary accuracy, although recent scholarship comparing photographs of Cézanne's scenes to his versions of them makes useful inferences about the basis of fact.[1] Most critics agree with Meyer Schapiro that "the visible world is not simply represented on Cézanne's canvas. It is recreated through strokes of color, among which are many that we cannot identify with an object and yet are necessary for the harmony of the whole."[2] But that phrase "recreated" needs to be examined. It means seeing things in a particular way and also making more than one interpretation of the same thing.

A number of critics have tried to deal with Hemingway's ideas about visual and verbal art. One attempt concludes that "Indian Camp" is constructed around "cyclical events" and repeated motifs.[3] Another argues that the reiteration of natural forms in "Big Two-Hearted River" can be traced to specific work like Cézanne's "The Poplars" and "Farmyard at Auvers."[4] A basic book on the subject, Emily Watts's *Ernest Hemingway and the Arts,* has a chapter on landscape that goes fairly deeply into the connection between painting and writing. It too notes the quality of reiteration, with

Paul Cézanne (French, 1839–1906), *Rocks in the Forest,* 1890s, Oil on canvas; 28⅞ × 36⅜ in. (73.3 × 92.4 cm): The Metropolitan Museum of Art, H. O. Havemeyer Collection, Bequest of Mrs. H. O. Havemeyer, 1929 (29.100.194). All Rights Reserved, The Metropolitan Museum of Art

characters in a number of works being attracted to the same qualities of (perceived) nature.[5] Certain landscapes "remain a constant" in the fiction.[6]

Hemingway acknowledged connections between his own work and visual art, especially that of Cézanne. The Lillian Ross interview at the Metropolitan Museum of Art in 1949 is often adduced:

> After we reached the Cézannes and Degas and the other Impressionists, Hemingway became more and more excited, and discoursed on what each artist could do and how and what he had learned from each. . . . Hemingway spent several minutes looking at Cézanne's "Rocks—Forest of Fontainbleau." "This is what we try to do in writing, this and this, and the woods, and the rocks we have to climb over," he said. "Cézanne is my painter, after the early painters. . . . I

can make a landscape like Mr. Paul Cézanne. I learned how to make
a landscape from Mr. Paul Cézanne by walking through the Luxembourg Museum a thousand times."[7]

Reiteration and sequence dominate the statement. Hemingway addresses a
painter and also painters before him. He refers to works behind this particular work that necessarily affect it. He implies familiarity with the way
that a particular school of painting turns and returns to its subjects. Even
his language is reiterative, although Ross does not pursue the definition of
"this . . . this and this." When Hemingway says he walked through the
museum "a thousand times" the repetition—which is fairly startling—
draws no blood. She treats it as an exaggeration, but it is meant as evidence
that he saw the same thing in necessarily different ways.

   The subject is itself a reiteration. There were many other studies of this
and related subjects. The rocks of Fontainebleau were part of an immense
body of work redone in order to capture as many aspects of landscape as
possible. In chronological order and keyed to the catalog of John Rewald:
*Rochers à l'Estaque; Dans le Parc du Château Noir; Rochers et Branches à
Bibémus; Sous Bois Devant les Grottes au-dessus du Château Noir; Rochers et
Arbres; Intérieur de Forêt; Pins et Rochers; Arbres et Rochers dans le Parc du
Château Noir; Rochers Près des Grottes au-dessus du Château Noir.* This list
does not include related subjects like the rock formations of the Mont
Sainte-Victoire paintings. The forms of "the woods, and the rocks" were
constantly reworked by Cézanne. These forms and certain others were
continuously reinvented by Hemingway.[8] So this notorious reference to
Rocks—Forest of Fontainebleau is not an allusion to a single view. The scene
was redrawn and repainted, part of an unending series of versions in pencil,
oils, and watercolors. Landscape scenes are variations on a central subject—
and even titles are reiterations. This could not have been unknown to
Hemingway.

   It may not be possible to pursue Hemingway's reference to the second
element of the painting, those "woods" that frame the rocks. John Rewald's
catalog, Lionello Venturi's *Cézanne,* and the Museum of Modern Art's
Cézanne: The Late Work list too many paintings on this subject to identify
Hemingway's allusions with any confidence.[9] He did not specify and Ross
did not pursue the immense number of versions of Cézanne's most essen-

tial element of landscape, the trees that provide vertical forms for the Fontainebleau painting. There are, for example: *L'Estaque; L'Estaque—Rochers, Pins et Mer; Marroniers et Ferme du Jas de Bouffan;* the many versions of *Sous-Bois; Les Grandes Arbres; Le Grand Pin; L'Allée à Chantilly; Dans la Forêt de Fontainebleau.* However, one reiterated subject in Cézanne can be traced because Hemingway invoked it a number of times and made it recognizably part of his own *language* as well as landscape.

The Cézannes that I have in mind among many others are *Maisons au Bord d'une Route; La Route Tournante* (1881); *Le Tournante de Route Près de Valhermeil; La Route Tournante à la Roche-Guyon; La Montagne Sainte-Victoire au Grand Pin; La Route en Provence; La Route Tournante en Sous-Bois; La Route Tournante (1904); Matinée de Printemps à Saint-Antonin;* and *La Route Tournante en Haut du Chemin des Lauves.* To these must be added numerous views of farms and towns, and, always, the series of paintings of Mont Sainte-Victoire. Cézanne's late landscapes—"curves in the road"—have been called new visions of nature.[10] Perhaps the issue left unpursued by the Ross interview—what, after all, was Hemingway referring to when he said that he had "learned" something of immense importance?—can be clarified. Evidently, one thing learned was the art of reiteration: "In the . . . *Mont Sainte-Victoire* series. . . . variations, studied like successive geological strata, grew out of Cézanne's ceaseless experimentation with the theme. They stem also from the different centering of the subject, which Cézanne insisted upon considering from every possible angle (left, right, forward, backward, high, low), according to the position in which he placed himself. The theme became a pretext for variations whose multiplicity distanced him from the concrete object."[11]

The central location for these ideas is in Hemingway's work of the twenties. Here is the opening of "The Three-Day Blow":

> The rain stopped as Nick turned into the road that went up through the orchard. The fruit had been picked and the fall wind blew through the bare trees. . . . The road came out of the orchard on to the top of the hill. There was the cottage, the porch bare, smoke coming from the chimney. In back was the garage, the chicken coop and the second-growth timber like a hedge against the woods behind.

The big trees swayed far over in the wind as he watched. It was the first of the autumn storms.[12]

Any reading of this necessarily begins, as the *Oxford English Dictionary* puts it, by "aiming at a close reproduction of nature."[13] We account for the realities of the scene. We relate the scene to its ostensible subject—in my view, incorrectly. Not only does the mode tell us something, but even more directly, the passage has embedded in it a number of allusions to the landscapes of Cézanne. The phrase "on top of the road" translates part of the title of *Le Mont Sainte-Victoire au-dessus de la Route du Tholonet* and also of *Maison près d'un tournant en haut du Chemin des Lauves.*[14] The phrase "the road came out of the orchard on to the top of the hill" not only contains the language of many titled paintings but is seen from their perspective. The phrase "the big trees" that "swayed far over in the wind" is literal Cézanne, as in the pencil and watercolor *Les Grands Arbres,* the oil *Les grandes arbres au Jas du Bouffon,* and a number of drawings. As for the second part of Hemingway's line, Lionello Venturi gave his own title to *Les Grandes Arbres—Bare Trees in the Fury of the Wind.*[15] That may be because Cézanne himself had in 1863 written a poem in connection with this subject containing the line "the tree shaken by the fury of the winds."[16]

Hemingway's opening lines are about more than one subject. In 1957, he completed a group of chapters for the book that was to become *A Moveable Feast.* He gave them to his wife Mary for typing—one of them told "how it was to be writing 'The Three-Day Blow' at a table in a café on the Place St.-Michel." But she was "disappointed to discover that the sketches contained so little that was straightforwardly autobiographical."[17] There is also very little that is straightforwardly documentary. In the section of *A Moveable Feast* that Carlos Baker describes, Hemingway writes that "in Paris I could write about Michigan." He meant that literally: "I was writing about up in Michigan and since it was a wild, cold, blowing day it was that sort of day in the story." Scholars are aware that he links the writing of the stories of this period to Paris and especially to Impressionism, but all readers will find it useful to get his own sense of connection: "I could walk through the gardens and then go to the Musée du Luxembourg where the great paintings were that have now mostly been transferred to the Louvre and the Jeu de Paume. I went there nearly every day for the Cézannes and to see the Manets and the Monets and the other Impressionists that I had first come to know about in the Art Institute of Chicago. I was learning something from the painting of Cézanne that made writing simple true sentences far from enough to make the stories have the dimensions that I was trying to put in them."[18]

Possibly more than technique was involved. Hemingway came to Cézanne at a time when Cézanne's stock was very high. Roger Fry had in 1914 called him "the Christopher Columbus of a new continent of form."[19] By 1927, when Fry's enormously influential book on Cézanne appeared, he was understood to be not only the leading post-Impressionist but also a world historical figure. *Fry himself was seen to be such a figure.*[20] Woolf's chapter on "The Post-Impressionists" in her biography of Roger Fry is an important part of the intellectual history of the early twentieth century. It covers his role in organizing, presenting—and reviewing—the great exhibitions of 1910 and 1912; even more importantly, it establishes his role in the transformation of artistic values. Fry, in fact, coined the term *post-Impressionism*. He mediated between collectors and artists; his writings influenced the public; and he was the single greatest influence on the next generation of English painters, critics, collectors, and reviewers. His central point was revaluation: Cézanne's achievement had been not to register appearance but to depict "a new and definite reality." Fry's summary applies to Hemingway's own practice: Cézanne and his school constructed their works imaginatively "with something of the same vividness as the things of actual life appeal to our practical activities."[21] The issue of representation through impression had never been only a matter of form.

Woolf believes that Fry's book on Cézanne was his most significant work, both for author and subject. She states that the theme of this book is the definition of artistic identity opposed to received opinion. She cites Fry on "the double story" of Cézanne, that is, his creating a technique and then becoming "the great protagonist of individual prowess against the herd."[22] So when we say that anyone might have been influenced by Cézanne or ideas about him in the intervening period, we necessarily mean that viewers came to the painter through ideas generated by his leading critic. What were some of those ideas? First, the painter's intellectualism was an important part of his total effect. Second, he provided a new kind of technical language for art. Third, the artist was himself a model for independent thought. Here is Fry on the late work, those landscapes so much admired by Hemingway:

> A picture belonging to M. Vollard . . . represents a road plunging from the immediate foreground into a wood of poplars, through which we surmise the presence of a rock face, which rises up behind and dominates the tree tops. . . . the more one looks the more do these dispersed indications begin to play together, to compose rhythmic phrases which articulate the apparent confusion, till at last all seems to come together to the eye into an austere and impressive architectural construction, which is all the more moving in that it emerges from this apparent chaos. It is perhaps in works like these that Cézanne reveals the extraordinary profundity of his imagination. He seems in them to attain to heights of concentration and elimination of all that is not pure plastic idea, which still outrange our pictorial apprehension. . . . the completest revelation of his spirit may be found in these latest creations.[23]

There are certain essentials: the motif of the road, the organization of detail into harmony, the warning that there are elements in his work that outrange our "pictorial apprehension." Above all, there is the conception of landscape as a dominant idea. I will return to these points after considering the more fundamental matter of representation.

Pavel Machotka has gone to archives and also, so far as they can be known, to Cézanne's locations. He has collected photographs of the sites and taken new ones from approximate perspectives. His reconstruction tries to account for the season and time of day of the original; change, damage, and natural cycles in the sites; and differing versions of the same scene. The reasons he gives for the project are helpful for Hemingway's own reiteration: chief among them that "more than one painting" is needed to produce coherence of idea or motif—and to be faithful to the variations of nature.[24] A single motif requires many versions. The idea was often restated in letters and interviews. That needs to be balanced against literary-critical presumptions. Hemingway scholars have tried to examine his landscape in terms of fidelity to "place." Robert W. Lewis sees "place" first of all as recognizable terrain. He concentrates on Hemingway's local knowledge and on the primacy of fact in any given description of city or country.[25] But he acknowledges also that such description is not a matter of documentation. "Place" is always modified by idea.[26]

That is a useful context for the opening of Hemingway's "The Three-Day Blow" in which the *route tournant* comes over a hill to a particular terrain. Getting there, we see the scene—but in a delimited way: "There was the cottage, the porch bare, smoke coming from the chimney. In back was the garage, the chicken coop and the second-growth timber like a hedge against the woods behind" (115). The usual descriptives are not there. There are no colors in this most important part of the opening. There is form but no draftsmanship—a trait in Cézanne much criticized by those who came after Roger Fry. Two things become apparent, the first that this passage is about perception not place; the second that it is seen in black and white. This is a drawing, not a painting, pencil without the usual watercolor. There is another perspective: "They stood together, looking out across the country, down over the orchard, beyond the road, across the lower fields and the woods of the point to the lake. The wind was blowing straight down the lake. They could see the surf along Ten Mile point." Here too there is the total absence of color—and no attempt to differentiate, describe, or compare objects within the scene. The curving road has taken us to a familiar but at the same time unexpected place, a Michigan landscape seen in Impressionist terms.[27]

The terrain in Hemingway's stories and novels of the twenties is seen from the viewpoint of "curves in the road" arriving at (even, to borrow Fry's phrasing, plunging into) landscapes of the mind.[28] "Indian Camp" begins by following a road that winds through the woods, arriving finally at a point in back of the hills. In order to get where they are going, which is both a real and a metaphorical place, Nick and his father have to come "around a bend" toward an equivocal light (92). In "The Battler" Nick starts along a smooth roadbed "going out of sight around the curve" (129). In "Big Two-Hearted River," he walks along a road "climbing to cross the range of hills" that separates two realms (211). "The Three-Day Blow" begins with a road that appears and disappears, going up through an orchard then "to the top of the hill" (115). In "In Another Country" the roads wind across land and water but recurve to meet and "always . . .

you crossed a bridge across a canal to enter the hospital" (267). The road in "An Alpine Idyll" stops at a cemetery, then climbs and twists into the hills where anything can happen. The motif is at its most dominant in the middle chapters of *The Sun Also Rises* where the *route tournante* takes us not only into the Spanish Pyrenees but into Cézanne's world of color and forms: "For a while the country was much as it had been; then, climbing all the time, we crossed the top of a Col, the road winding back and forth on itself, and then it was really Spain."[29]

The *route tournante* has had different kinds of histories in visual art and literature. Sometimes they coalesce. In art history, roads have a technical function of separating the planes of a landscape. One example—startling in its delineation of limits—is Armand Guillaumin's *The Outskirts of Paris,* done about 1874. If ever one wants to see a road "winding back and forth on itself" while fragmenting nature into parcels, this is the oil painting to view. Yet here technique and meaning shade into each other: about half the painting is taken up by the recurved road, which speaks either to a pleasing sense of geometry or to a baffled sense of the segregation of things natural behind barriers.[30] The sense of a division of realms is strong: between men and nature, between the artist and the object before him. In Hemingway, the winding road is by no means a still, formal part of a described scene. It is an entry into a divided realm. The point has been made forcibly: in his own analysis of *Rocks at Fontainebleau* Meyer Schapiro points out that "there is a similar landscape in the writing of Flaubert. . . . In his great novel, *The Sentimental Education,* he describes the same forest of Fontaine-bleau as the setting of two lovers who have left Paris for the peace of nature during the convulsions of 1848: 'The path zigzags between the stunted pines under the rocks with angular profiles. . . . But the fury of their chaos makes one think rather of volcanos, deluges and great forgotten cata-clysms.'"[31] Schapiro says that this scene from the novel is even more dis-turbing than Paris. It reminds us of natural disorder—which becomes coupled with our own sense of inevitable human disorder.

The openings of both "Indian Camp" and "The Battler" are illuminated by the following passage about the "limited access of entry" into some of Cézanne's *routes tournantes:* "A clear visual path is frustrated, in the first composition, by the restless violence of the overlapping planes formed by the rocks; in the second, by the aggressive jutting of the rock at the framing edge and by the densely grouped, multi-colored foliage, which forms another barrier across the road and denies the eye a place to rest; in the third, by the ominously insistent intrusion of the trees and their branches into the line of sight."[32] "Indian Camp" has this kind of topography, with its access of entry going "through a meadow that was soaking wet with dew" along a trail that first "went into the woods" and then to a "road that ran back into the hills" (91). The words replicate Cézanne's titles; the terrain replicates his scenes. Hemingway uses the road—which, in order to arrive in the frame, even "came around a bend"—to repeat motifs of Impressionist perception. Boundaries are in fact barriers. Volumes are in sharp contrast, with the shapeless and organic completely unclarified.[33] The road, which is after all a figure of more than one kind of perspective, does not grant "access" to the meadow, woods, or hills. The geometry of culture does not appear to have "access" to the irregularity of nature, and so the burden of the story has been prefigured.

In this story, Hemingway raises a large question about the separation of things knowable and unknowable. He works with the conflict of visual components. His mountains and forest edges are not only volumes and planes but lines of limitation. Isaiah Berlin was later to use the concept of "access" in a related way. In a skeptical essay on the possibility of shaping reality, he concluded that there was no possibility of doing so. Some areas of the world—and also within the mind—would always be unreachable: "The belief that somewhere there exists a solution for every problem, though it may be concealed and difficult of access . . . is the major assumption that is presupposed in the whole of Western thought. Moral and political questions, in this respect, did not differ from others."[34] Berlin thinks that while everything is open to inquiry, few things are permeable to it.[35] It was Wittgenstein of course who set the rules about limits of understanding. Here is his opinion—it is a memorable one—of Bertrand Russell's confusion of certainties: "Russell's works should be bound in two colours . . . those dealing with mathematical logic in red—and all students of philosophy should read them; those dealing with ethics and politics in blue—and no one should be allowed to read them."[36] The explanation of experience has its limits, and they are quickly reached. That matters greatly as a context for a story full of questions without answers.

The idea of access denied applies to Hemingway. The premise of roads and also of inquiries is that they go somewhere. *Routes tournantes* invariably fail to reach certain symbolic objects on their horizon. They reach but cannot penetrate the barriers of rocks, woods, mountains. In "Indian Camp" Nick asks the question "Where are we going?" and the answer is necessarily qualified. Perhaps it can be provided from "The Battler," in which we are "a long way off from anywhere." There is always "the curve" and, as usual, it goes "out of sight" from foreground to background (129). Once again there are the undefined volumes of woods and swamp. These make their own demands on interpretation. (A recent history of the novel makes the point that "the place between water and land functions . . . as a threshold. Its presence signifies the necessity of passing from one state to another.")[37] The roadway devolves from track to trail to a path "at the edge of the trees" (130). We move from perspective to a point beyond viewing, and from technique to meaning—we now know the tendency of the story, from known to unknown. It is characteristic in Hemingway to begin on a straight road or roadway and then to experience an entirely different kind of locus of movement—and also of the mind.

"The Battler" begins with Nick being thrown off a freight train and walking, tired, cold, and hungry, along the railroad tracks. We begin with straight lines, which is to say within the Western mind. But Nick is surrounded by dark woods and impenetrable swamps, the psychic meanings of which are sufficiently clear. When Nick gets to the campfire that he has seen from the railroad tracks he finds a man called Ad who has been wrecked by his life. Ad has been in the ring, and he took a good punch. The trouble is, he took too many of them. But the ring may not have been what broke him. The meeting is something so different from Nick's orderly middle-class past that it makes such a past itself unreal. He expects logic in experience; Ad Francis is there to show that chaos is as likely as order. He has been a heroic figure—"I could take it," he says, "Don't you think I could take it, kid?" (131)—but the ring has deformed him, made him, as he says, "crazy." He has been married, or pretended to be married, to a woman who may—or may not—have been his sister. He welcomes Nick to the fire, then transparently tries to take Nick's knife in order to stab him. So we have Ad being crazy, incompatible reasons for it, and Ad wanting to kill Nick. It has been remarked often that in these stories Nick always learns something, but what he learns here is that there may not be any answers.

In the middle of it all, Bugs heats a skillet, and ham, eggs, and bread materialize: "As the skillet grew hot the grease sputtered and Bugs . . . turned the ham and broke eggs into the skillet, tipping it from side to side to baste the eggs with the hot fat" (133). One kind of detail belongs to the constancy of nature: fire heats, ham slices are held on bread by gravity, bread picks up gravy by osmosis, eggs run because liquids seek their own level. The laws of mechanics are working, but a second kind of detail seems less Newtonian: Bugs tells a wonderful story-within-the-story about how Ad Francis went mad, gives Nick more food and coffee, then calmly hits Ad with an antique blackjack that has seen a lot of use. He is precise, just putting Ad to sleep with a well-placed tap. Nick leaves the camp, looks backward, sees Bugs waking his friend up and giving him some more coffee. The story moves relativistically from one set of boundaries to another. They have no intersection.

The most sustained of Hemingway's landscapes of the twenties are those in *The Sun Also Rises*. All are approached from railroad tracks, roads, trails, and paths that circle and rise and then disappear:

There were wide fire-gaps cut through the pines, and you could look up them like avenues and see wooded hills way off. . . . then we were out in the country, green and rolling, and the road climbing all the time. . . . then the road turned off and commenced to climb and we were going way up close along a hillside, with a valley below and hills stretched off back toward the sea. . . . then, climbing all the time, we crossed the top of a Col, the road winding back and forth on itself. . . . and the road ran down to the right, and we saw a whole new range of mountains. . . . and the road went on, very white and straight ahead, and then lifted to a little rise. . . . away off you could see the plateau of Pamplona rising out of the plain, and the walls of the city, and the great brown cathedral and the broken skyline of the other churches. . . . the road slanting up steeply and dustily with shade-trees on both sides, and then levelling out. . . . The road climbed up into the hills and left the rich grain-fields below . . . and the hills were rocky and hard-baked clay furrowed by the rain. We came around a curve into a town, and on both sides opened out a sudden green valley. . . . Far back the fields were squares of green and brown on the hillsides. Making the horizon were the brown mountains. They were strangely shaped. As we climbed higher the horizon kept changing. As the bus ground slowly up the road we could see other mountains coming up in the south. Then the road came over the crest, flattened out, and went into a forest. It was a forest of cork oaks, and the sun came through the trees in patches . . . and ahead of us was a rolling green plain, with dark mountains behind it.[38]

Hemingway's *routes tournantes* are more allusive than we may think. I have by no means covered all of his versions of the road winding through Spain—while it simultaneously traverses the landscapes of Cézanne. It goes through a particular part of Cézanne: I think that the best way to get at Hemingway's reiterations of the *route tournante* is through the Mont Sainte-Victoire paintings.

Arguing from technique, Pavel Machotka calls the ten canvases Cézanne did on this subject between 1902 and 1906 his culminating work. They provide the volumes and also the green and brown (ocher) in Hemingway's own version. They provide the translations from planes of entry and of view. They have, as Cézanne himself noted, the property of never having colors "join at the edges." They alternate "meadows" and "full sun." Above all, they create a succession of views with new understanding of a landscape reached at different points. But the consideration of technique inevitably reaches a point of meaning, and Machotka concludes that just as his own photographs of the scene are inadequate, so is the argument from technique. This is a culminating series of works because nothing else has managed in this way to translate space onto canvas.[39]

The "space" in question is the distant view of the mountain made accessible, *but only to a limited extent,* by roads that rise and curve and disappear. Toward the end of his life, in 1901, Cézanne bought a modest property halfway up the hill of Les Lauves north of Aix. Here is where he spent the days making the last paintings of Mont Sainte-Victoire. He rarely changed his perspective of the mountain but kept on painting it from different angles, at different times, and in different colors. No single image represents a final view of the subject. None of these paintings is ever able to resolve—and none of them care to provide—any final interpretation of the scene. The components of these views are invariably earth and sky: The entry into these components is invariably through *routes tournantes* like those "countless gently climbing, descending, and curving roads with hills in the background" around Les Lauves.[40] The roads are everywhere, yet there are in all these canvases areas that cannot be fully explained. On this the painter was adamant, even stating that a blank space would be preferable to inserting something that would fake comprehension. Landscape was by no means open to visual understanding—we recall Fry's statement that it might "outrange our pictorial apprehension."

In a letter to his son in 1906 Cézanne remarked "that as a painter I am becoming more clear-sighted before nature, but with me the realization of my sensations is always painful. I cannot attain the intensity that is unfolded before my senses. I do not have the magnificent richness of coloring that animates nature."[41] The solution is to keep repainting certain motifs at different times and from different angles. The same subject needs to be repeated in the hope that at some point its meaning will reveal itself. During an interview in the same year, 1906, Cézanne took out a number of paintings from all over his house and "followed the limits of the various planes on his canvases. He showed exactly how far he had succeeded in suggesting the depth and where the solution had not yet been found."[42] Implicit is the idea that a painting is not simply exposition. It concerns information withheld. Another interview conducted by Joachim Gasquet (printed in Paris in 1926) finds Cézanne discoursing at some length about the point at which description may—or may not—be adequate to the subject:

> You see, a motif is this. . . . (He put his hands together . . . drew them apart, ten fingers open, then slowly, very slowly brought them together again, clasped them, squeezed them tightly, meshing them.) That's what one should try to achieve. . . . If one hand is held too high or too low, it won't work. Not a single link should be too slack, leaving a hole through which the emotion, the light, the truth can escape. You must understand that I work on the whole canvas, on everything at once. With one impulse, with undivided faith, I ap-

proach all the scattered bits and pieces. . . . Everything we see falls apart, vanishes, doesn't it? Nature is always the same, but nothing in her that appears to us lasts. . . . What is there underneath? Maybe nothing. Maybe everything. Everything, you understand! So I bring together her wandering hands. . . . I take something at right, something at left, here, there, everywhere, her tones, her colors, her nuances, I set them down, I bring them together. . . . They form lines. They become objects, rocks, trees, without my planning. They take on volume, value. . . . But if there is the slightest distraction, if I fail just a little bit, above all if I interpret too much one day, if today I am carried away by a theory which runs counter to that of yesterday, if I think while I paint, if I meddle, whoosh! Everything goes to pieces.[43]

To be aware of this interview is to put the Ross interview into perspective. A relentless empiricism marks both Cézanne's work and Hemingway's. Iteration means the discovery of an identity more complex than any single given statement about it. As expected, Cézanne is concerned with two main issues: constant reinterpretation and the extraction of meaning from technique. We are prepared to think of the rocks and trees in their landscapes as real and also as symbolic entities. Both conclude that one may find either "everything" or "nothing" in a scene. The remark, like Hemingway's observation to Ross about "what we try to do," is elliptical: writing and painting can succeed and also fail in depiction. And even when they do succeed in their statement, there are barriers to cognition.

Gasquet took down Cézanne's opinion that the issue of painting a landscape finally becomes one of adequate "language." Painting, according to Cézanne, was the "deciphering" of a "text." The process, in fact, is that of establishing "two parallel texts" of visualization and the statement of meaning. In the Ross interview Hemingway talks about paintings and motifs; here Cézanne talks about language and texts. Both imply that the study of terrain and composition exceeds the mastery of topography. I have not cited everything stated or claimed by Cézanne, but the more one looks at this 1926 interview, the better Hemingway looks at the Met.

In summarizing the last landscapes, Meyer Schapiro begins with technique, emphasizing the importance of changing colors from point to point and making sense out of separated details. Then he adds that "the distant landscape resolves to some degree the strains of the foreground world. . . . dualities that remain divided, tense, and unstable in the observer's space." His conclusion makes sense when applied to a particular moment in *The Sun Also Rises*. As Schapiro points out, a kind of double drama is in process, that of the eye's movement through terrain and that of building a kind of intellectual "harmony." The scene has "externalized" something not easily articulated. Momentarily, control has been achieved over experience.[44] Both Machotka and Schapiro—and the many art historians cited by Rewald in his definitive study—find the Mont Sainte-Victoire iterations to have considerable spiritual depth, even unstated religious feeling. When Jake and Bill finally reach water in the mountains, they make an embarrassed but effective iteration of their own, retelling Genesis within a landscape by the banks of a stream. In the scene, a road rises into the woods and then turns in its curving way across the fields. Schapiro states of "Road at Chantilly" that the path through the trees seems to be "a modest, unlikely theme."[45] But it is everywhere in Cézanne and Hemingway.

6
Orwell
The Future of Progress

One can't deal with the Idea of Progress without including George Orwell because he ended it. But was his effect merely political? It seemed so—readers behind the Iron Curtain were "amazed that a writer who never lived in Russia should have so keen a perception into its life."[1] Originally meant as praise, this now implies that *Nineteen Eighty-Four* assumes importance from a subject that has disappeared. That is not necessarily a disqualification—literature outlasts its political subjects. But a dilemma remains if this particular novel is adduced *because* of the political system it has outlived. The issue is territoriality: many on the Left see Orwell as an ideological turncoat, while "American neoconservatives . . . claim him as a precursor." Many who do not read him wonder what Orwell might think "if he were alive today."[2] The discussion of his work is connected, overwhelmingly, to the beliefs of his critics. It is as if we praised Shakespeare for his support of either Lancaster or York.

I have a different set of questions about his work. Some of my questions proceed from Freud's conclusions on actual order and its mythology. Not long before the publication of *Nineteen Eighty-Four,* he wrote that "civilization is a process in the service of Eros, whose purpose is to combine single human individuals, and after that families, then races, peoples and nations, into one great unity."[3] The view is larger than politics, and what matters most, I think, is Freud's understanding of that great unity. I have other particular texts in mind, and I think it indisputable that they were on Orwell's mind.

Nineteen Eighty-Four is about the chief city of Airstrip One, a province of Oceania. But a place in fiction, like Pemberley or Laputa or Vanity Fair, is in part an idea. The story resists technological futurism—there are no spaceships or platinum suits with diagonal zippers. It is thoroughly conventional; few other works about our lives are so permeated by the smell of boiled cabbage. Although set in the future, it seems to require knowledge about the past. The story is not intelligible without the historical presence of Lenin, Stalin, and Trotsky. At another remove, we need to know about events of the twentieth century. But we also need to know certain texts and dialogues. We are, I think, intended to recognize themes like the topos of awakening into intellectual and spiritual life. Winston Smith shares the awakening experience not only with the prisoners of the Ministry of Love but with Lear, Kurtz and Marlowe, and Gregor Samsa. *Nineteen Eighty-Four* is a very *literary* book because it is full of echoes of other books. Some of its echoes go back farther than we may think. To read Orwell's *Collected Essays, Journalism and Letters* is to be overwhelmed by the names of authors and the titles of books. His own writing is a library of allusions to Arnold, Baudelaire, Belloc, Carlyle, Dickens, Eliot, Flaubert, Gissing, Hardy, Lawrence, Powell, Shakespeare, Waugh, and others the full mention of whom would take some time. He read everything and quarreled with most of it. One part of his reading became part of his writing. We know that he read the classics because he complained in such detail about having to read them. When he was at St. Cyprian's (the school in "Such, Such Were the Joys") they were force-fed to him. In order for the school to make a reputation, the scholarship boys were bullied into brilliance. They had to become encyclopedias of Latin and Greek, "crammed with learning as cynically as a goose is crammed for Christmas."[4] Orwell wrote of his involuntary mastery of the classics, "looking back, I realise that I then worked harder than I have ever done since."[5] It is a fairly strong remark from the author of *Down and Out in Paris and London.*

Orwell's favorite reading on summer mornings at school when he was temporarily free from his own set of academic guardians included the novels of H. G. Wells. Wells's early science fiction was built around Darwinism. The strength of *The Time Machine* lies in its adaptation of evolution, a process that Wells understood might go in reverse. His novel begins with the triumph of technology but proceeds to ever more primitive and lifeless future times. Orwell found some of these themes useful to his story—but he did not concentrate on scientific entropy, writing instead about the entropy of ideas. He begins, necessarily, at the beginning, with Aristotle's *Politics,* which contains many observations on tyranny.

Aristotle is visibly present in Orwell: the fifth book of the *Politics* concerns revolution and its causes—and also its prevention. It describes a divided society of aristocracy and "masses." That society is penetrated by informers, spies, eavesdroppers—even by "secret police." The *Politics* analyzes the state's intention to keep its citizens poor. It describes the state's opposition to all other social units, especially the family. It refers to the calculated public promotion of hatred. It talks about war as an extension of domestic politics. Above all, it is about the attack on what Aristotle called the "spirit" of the polis. His argument is existential: "Men tend to become revolutionaries from circumstances connected with their private lives."[6] Aristotle writes, in fact, *that private life may be the main issue.* We see this idea translated by Orwell into novelistic episodes (although there are other classical sources for the attack on private life).[7] Aristotle describes the tyrannical practices of preventing private gatherings, requiring citizens to appear in public, getting "regular information about every man's sayings and doings." Politics, as in *Nineteen Eighty-Four,* has an essential psychological component—"men are not so likely to speak their minds if they go in fear of a secret police" (245). The primary end of unjust rule is to render citizens "incapable of action" (246). Airstrip One may well be Moscow in 1946 or London in 1984, but it is also an idea derived from a text. Except for stylistic differences, it would be hard to tell whether Orwell or Ernest Barker, Aristotle's translator, wrote the following: "Tyranny is never overthrown until men can begin to trust one another; and this is the reason why tyrants are always at outs with the good. They feel that good men are doubly dangerous to their authority—dangerous, first, in thinking it shame to be governed as if they were slaves; dangerous, again, in their spirit of mutual and general loyalty, and in their refusal to betray one another or anybody else" (246).

In the *Politics,* virtue never remains a matter of individual morality. The virtuous man is an "outstanding" citizen—that is to say, he represents public values. Because public and private lives are inseparable this man is the natural object of tyranny. He need not be in active opposition to the state. It suffices that his excellence be visible. In Aristotle, such a man is a potential threat to political order. Winston Smith seems unheroic in terms of *ethos*. But he must be seen against the possibilities of all other characters. He is, to begin, far more honest. He is capable of independent thought. He loves what is beautiful—an idea that begins as a curiosity in this story and ends as a kind of necessary cause. In his world, small differences constitute large meanings. If Winston Smith's character did not constitute an Aristotelian threat to illicit power then the following dialogue would not have been written:

> "And you consider yourself morally superior to us, with our lies and our cruelty?"
> "Yes, I consider myself superior."[8]

This statement comes not before but after torture.

All outstanding men are potential criminals in the eyes of the state. Aristotle was much interested in a certain story about such citizens, mentioning it on three separate occasions in the *Politics*. It is about the appropriate penalty for excellence. By the time the story had reached him it had become a parable. The story is about the "advice which was offered by Periander to his fellow-tyrant Thrasybulus" about the best way to deal with those potential enemies, the "outstanding citizens" of the commonwealth (237). It is one of the great political anecdotes—here I quote the more developed version of Herodotus:

> On one occasion he sent a herald to ask Thrasybulus what mode of government it was safest to set up in order to rule with honour. Thrasybulus led the messenger without the city, and took him into a field of corn, through which he began to walk, while he asked him again and again concerning his coming from Corinth, ever as he went breaking off and throwing away all such ears of corn as over-topped the rest. In this way he went through the whole field, and destroyed the richest and best part of the crop.[9]

The bewildered messenger returns home, and it is left to the imagination to interpret the meaning. The version of Herodotus reverses the asking and giving of advice, but he has clearly provided the essential strategy: cut off the tallest heads. The *Politics* takes its point of departure for the study of tyranny from this story. Orwell has translated not only event but character— Winston differs from the rest not because of civic merit but because of his honesty, sensibility, and intellectual stubbornness. As both he and O'Brien acknowledge, he is indeed "superior."

Aristotle's discussion of the state does not rest on constitutional rule or even on political ends. He is focused on the experience of daily life. His understanding of the "traditional" policies of tyranny is encyclopedic, but the text is also a catalog of all those policies directed "against everything likely to produce the two qualities of mutual confidence and a high spirit" (244). The statement seems oddly inexact, not philosophical. But it closely resembles Orwell's conception of policy and citizenship in *Nineteen Eighty-Four*. One of the great ends of the authoritarian state, Aristotle argues, is to break the "spirit" of its citizens. His discussion of tyranny in Athens, Corinth, Sparta, and other places contains more than circumstance; he provides much psychological insight and also speculation. On one level the text concerns ruinous taxes, unjust laws, and inhuman penalties. On another, it is concerned with the destruction of what is intuitive in human character and free in human expression.

Aristotle writes of friendship, confidence, trust, feeling, and, above all, that matter of "spirit." He refers again and again to that term, coming back to it each time as the ultimate object of tyrannic power. He insists on the human necessity for association and describes the many forms that association takes. *Nineteen Eighty-Four* is also about association in all its forms: the sexual union, marriage, the formation of the family, the choice of friends, the consent of the community. Each of its episodes is in some exemplary way about the breakdown of human association. This is not a story of political resistance; one might say rather that it displays sensibility. It certainly does not describe the activity of a political cell. Winston's ideas of rebellion are never more than hopes or illusions. The narrative describes sexual and aesthetic consciousness; its central object is a piece of coral embedded in glass; its central act is the act of love.

How does the corrupt state think of itself, and how does it accomplish its desires? O'Brien, who likes to pose as a teacher in dialogue with the uninitiated, often mentions the theory and practice of oligarchy. For example, he tells Winston that this regime is "different from all the oligarchies of the past. . . . One does not establish a dictatorship in order to safeguard a revolution; one makes the revolution in order to establish the dictatorship. The object of persecution is persecution. The object of torture is torture. The object of power is power" (116). The focus now is on aberrant psychology, implied by Aristotle, highly developed in Orwell.[10]

O'Brien competes with all political theory before him. When he discusses oligarchy his version surpasses the classical definition, and when he discusses tyranny his version outdoes the pallid beginnings of injustice so far recorded. He has the trait, almost the tic, of comparing the future with the past. This guides the reader to understand that the development of social forms is in fact a devolution. What all previous books or documents say about the effect of tyranny on private life will be exceeded after the orgasm has been "abolished." The entire philosophical category of "private" life will also necessarily have been abolished. Aristotle tells us that men must live their private lives in public so that what they say and whom they say it to are under scrutiny. In fact, under tyranny, all citizens must literally be under the eye of government: the forced exhibition of private life "is meant to give the ruler a peep-hole into the actions of his subjects, and to inure them to humility by a habit of daily slavery" (244). Orwell allows O'Brien to show how previous political theory has been disarmed by its own limits of imagination and, possibly, by the last aftereffects of habitual decency.

When we read the list of state activities provided by Aristotle, we can see that it provides Orwell with the skeletal structure for the events of his novel:

A fourth line of policy is that of endeavouring to get regular information about every man's sayings and doings. This entails a secret police like the female spies employed at Syracuse, or the eavesdroppers sent by the tyrant Hiero to all social gatherings and public meetings. (Men are not so likely to speak their minds if they go in fear of a secret police; and if they do speak out, they are less likely to go undetected). Still another line of policy is to sow mutual distrust and

to foster discord between friend and friend; between people and no-
tables; between one section of the rich and another. Finally, a policy
pursued by tyrants is that of impoverishing their subjects. . . . The
imposition of taxes produces a similar result. . . . The same vein of
policy also makes tyrants war-mongers, with the object of keeping
their subjects constantly occupied and continually in need of a leader.
(244–45)

One grants that these ideas have passed into universal currency. After two
thousand years, they are to be found scattered from Machiavelli to Lenin.
But the mode of the novel is pointedly historical. O'Brien invokes past
tyrannies from Egypt to the Inquisition to National Socialism in order to
establish the primacy of the Party. Some historical references are traceable
to the *Politics:* one of the best ways to waste civic resources intentionally,
Aristotle writes, is to undertake useless public projects like "the building of
the Egyptian pyramids: another is the lavish offerings to temples" (245).
A text within Orwell's text, *The Theory and Practice of Oligarchical Collec-
tivism,* says that "it would be quite simple to waste the surplus labor of the
world by building temples and pyramids" (85). The advance in thinking
(O'Brien is always anxious to top his sources) consists of building such
things at great cost—and then doubling the waste by destroying them in
wars. Barker's midcentury translation of Aristotle has it that under tyranny
it is customary "to increase the poverty of the tyrant's subjects and to cur-
tail their leisure" (245). In Orwell, O'Brien states that "leisure" must be
abolished because the "hierarchical" state is built upon "a basis of poverty" (84).
    The aim of power is to reduce citizens to slaves and, in the Barker trans-
lation, to conquer their innate "refusal to betray one another or anybody
else." The word "betray" is used many times in Orwell. It does not mean
giving up political secrets under interrogation. Rather, it means giving
up mutual trust, loyalty, confidence, and love—all of which are essential
civic qualities in Aristotle. The unjust polity intends *above all,* according
to the *Politics,* to break the human "spirit." Before his torture, Winston
distinguishes between confession and betrayal. That follows the implications of the *Politics* because, while confession is a political act, betrayal is
directed against human association. Julia, measurably less conscious than

Winston, begins this particular exchange by saying that "Everybody always confesses. You can't help it. They torture you." Here is Winston's answer:

> I don't mean confessing. Confession is not betrayal. What you say or do doesn't matter; only feelings matter. If they could make me stop loving you—that would be the real betrayal. (73–74)

The distinction is based on Aristotle, signifying that the unjust polity internalizes order. By preventing personal relationship it assures political control.

Under torture, Winston betrays "everybody and everything"—with one exception. That is to say, he confesses. Because confession is not betrayal, he remains, after the first stage of torture, partly immune to the power of the state. The measure of his character is not only that he knows this but admits it:

> "You have whimpered for mercy, you have betrayed everybody and everything. Can you think of a single degradation that has not happened to you?"
>
> Winston had stopped weeping, though the tears were still oozing out of his eyes. He looked up at O'Brien.
>
> "I have not betrayed Julia," he said.
>
> O'Brien looked down at him thoughtfully. "No," he said, "no; that is perfectly true. You have not betrayed Julia." (121)

A good reader of the *Politics,* O'Brien knows the distinction that Winston has raised. He reserves punishment for him of the kind that will assuredly "break" his "spirit." O'Brien's phrase "you have betrayed everybody and everything" needs to stand against Aristotle's phrase "the refusal to betray one another or anybody else." There is an answering passage to the above, after Winston has returned from Room 101 of the Ministry of Love:

> "I betrayed you," she said baldly.
>
> "I betrayed you," he said. (129)

"After that," Julia explains, "you don't feel the same toward the other person any longer." The words are those of Orwell; the ideas belong to Aristotle. When mutual trust, confidence, and love disappear, then the "spirit" has been broken. The only rival left to the power of the state has been betrayed.

During the course of his torture at the Ministry of Love, Winston discovers the motives of the Party. They seem not to belong at all to ordinary political ends—totalitarian states usually settle for obedience:

> Never again will you be capable of ordinary human feeling. Everything will be dead inside you. Never again will you be capable of love, or friendship, or joy of living, or laughter, or curiosity, or integrity. You will be hollow. We shall squeeze you empty, and then fill you with ourselves. (113)

At this point we depart from those who believe that *Nineteen Eighty-Four* is about actual totalitarian regimes—and, necessarily, from all those who defend or attack the novel because of their own political ideologies. It makes little sense to interpret the revelations that come about at the Ministry of Love as if they reflected political reality. We know rather a lot about twentieth-century totalitarianism after reading *The Destruction of European Jewry, The Origins of Totalitarianism,* and *The Gulag Archipelago.* These books do not suggest that the modern totalitarian state aims at anything more than the extinction of opposition. The KGB was not interested operationally in the feelings per se of dissidents. It used torture to beat people down and drugs to make them helpless or psychotic. Hannah Arendt summarizes the state's attitude toward political opposition: "Criminals are punished, undesirables disappear from the face of the earth; the only trace which they leave behind is the memory of those who knew and loved them, and one of the most difficult tasks of the secret police is to make sure that even such traces will disappear together with the condemned man."[11] And of course it must be so: in a nation of 250 million prisoners it does no good to have the worst offenders on parole. The business of the secret police is to eradicate them, not change their minds. Totalitarianism deals with large social groups. The job of the Gestapo or KGB was "not to discover crimes, but to be on hand when the government decides to arrest a certain category of the population."[12] Secret police are bureaucrats, not romantics. *Nineteen Eighty-Four* misleads us if it suggests that we are speaking only of real political regimes. Secret police do not read books or worry about the past, although O'Brien spends a lot of time doing both. Secret police have the *opposite* of a philosophy, for they do whatever the leadership requires, even if it contradicts what they were told an hour before. In fact, as Hannah Arendt describes, the secret police find no trouble in doing some things clearly contradictory at the same time: awarding some poor devil of a bureaucrat a medal and putting him before the firing squad. Secret police are content with the appearance only of submission. They are themselves a bureaucracy and find perfection a time-wasting goal. What they want is compliance, not conversions.

There is then a *difference* between actual totalitarian strategy and that propounded by O'Brien. What does he want to accomplish? He gives us a transparently clear answer: the object of power is power. But by what tactic does the state attain that object? By making it difficult, even impossible, to believe in an alternative to its daily practices. How is such an alternative denied? By making daily life entirely arbitrary, subject not to historical or cultural norms but only to dictates; that is to say, by changing the definition of norms. That seems so *thinkable,* especially in a satire of intellectuals. Yet, order in personal life is as mythopoeic as any conception governing that life. It necessarily resists ideas and presents a special problem to the unanchored mind.

The politics of Orwell's novel have obscured its mythology. Freud's great point in *Civilization and Its Discontents*—the peroration to the sixth chapter—is that the agon of our civilization has always been more than political. Warring doctrines disguise the primal strategy of modifying human character and relationships. This was an important part of a subject much on Freud's mind, which he took to be the underlying message of folktales, fairy tales, and myth. And of literature itself.[13] Story in all of its variations poised life against power.

∼

When critics write of novels, they take account of dream and myth. When Freud writes of politics, he emphatically does the same. Freud consistently argues that the eternal project of despotism has never been mere political dominion. Its "dream" of absolute, psychological control had been renewed by 1930; the new fields of its operation were central and eastern Europe. It was not by chance "that the dream of a Germanic world-dominion called for antisemitism as its complement." And it was entirely logical "that the attempt to establish a new, communist civilization in Russia should find its psychological support in the persecution of the bourgeois." He added, "one only wonders, with concern, what the Soviets will do after they have wiped out their bourgeois."[14] "Persecution" is a more than political term, and in *Nineteen Eighty-Four* O'Brien states that—like power—it is its own object.

Civilization and Its Discontents was translated into English in 1930. It is not the only text of Freud that provides us with insights into the fundamental relationships of individuals to social groups. *The Future of An Illusion* (translated in 1928) defined "civilization" as minority control of a resistant majority through "possession of the means to power." In that book, Freud identified the central problem of rule as internalization, that is, implanting ideas within the minds of citizens.[15] Coercion was necessary to accomplish that because "education" alone can never erase our recalcitrant desires. The state cannot depend on voluntary renunciation of those desires because the capacity to do that varies from one person to another. As for the "mass" of men, they are hopelessly indifferent to ideas. (*The Future of An Illusion* concerns religion but implies politics: "these dangerous masses must be held down severely and kept most carefully away from any chance of intellectual awakening").[16] In *Civilization and Its Discontents*, Freud argues that progress is not possible because of the self-aggrandizing nature of government—and because of inherent human aggressiveness, which seeks out positions of authority. He developed the idea that "aggressivity and destructiveness" characterize social experience. And he dwelt on the ways in which a "sense of guilt" could be created within individuals to prevent their opposition to mindless dictates from above.[17] These things are included in his conception of political "power."

Like Freud, Orwell combined politics with the larger idea of power asserted over mind and body. He did not have lyrical talent, but the story of Julia and Winston is one of the great love stories of the century because we know what it means. Their love is what Freud called "a process in the service of Eros, whose purpose is to combine single human individuals." That seems formalistic, as does his notion of the progression from self through "families, then races, peoples and nations." The strength of Freud's idea, however, is that love cannot be attacked without attacking the natural order.

Is there such a thing? Isaiah Berlin wrote of the order that, "in one version or another, has dominated European thought since Plato . . . [and] has appeared in many forms and has generated many similes and allegories."[18] The most basic of these connected the planets, political realms, and the human body and soul. One needs to give these not-outworn *figurae* sufficient credit. Do the small subjects that Orwell writes about have more than tactile or nervous presence? Are they both things in themselves and also representations? Since its beginnings and in all of its times of trouble, the West has feared order's great opposite. It is usually depicted, and not only by Milton, as a combination of power and death. Orwell's novel refers to and is really built upon the most primitive of mysteries. It refers to the return to something so fearful that all Western mythology is about its transcendence. The biblical myth notwithstanding, that of the Pelasgian creation says, "In the beginning, Eurynome, the goddess of All Things, rose naked from chaos" and divided sea from sky. According to the myth of the Olympian creation, "At the beginning of all things Mother Earth emerged from Chaos"—and the work of Nature was to set all things in "due order, as they are now found."[19] According to Plato, "the divine order of the world" causes the philosopher "to reproduce that order in his soul." The great exception is despotism, more than a political conception, which wants to rule "over all mankind and heaven besides."[20] As to the nature of that rule, O'Brien's is only the second best-known speech in English on the subject. It seems possible that right and wrong can lose their names, and justice too; "Then everything includes itself in power. . . ."[21] *Troilus and Cressida* concludes that this constitutes a return to chaos.

Nineteen Eighty-Four is not about the gulag or the difference between constitutional and actual rights. It is about the nightmare of the West, a nightmare that has been sublimated by an endless sequence of meditations on the just society. When it tells us that the past is over it means that the dream of order and justice does not correspond to human actuality. *Civilization and Its Discontents* defines evil in these lines from Goethe, who was

Freud's own literary mentor: "*Denn alles, was entsteht / Ist wert, dass es zu Grunde geht*"—all that came from chaos must now be destroyed.[22] Freud bypassed the specific actions and doctrines of national politics, concluding that the "evolution of civilization" will always have to endure aggression in the form of attacks on libido and human association. It would have been quite simple to allude directly to doctrine and event. Instead, he described the psychology of power striving for "omnipotence."[23]

That has certain implications for the idea of progress. The end of *Civilization and Its Discontents* is deflationary: "For a wide variety of reasons, it is very far from my intention to express an opinion upon the value of human civilization. I have endeavoured to guard myself *against the enthusiastic prejudice which holds that our civilization is the most precious thing that we possess or could acquire and that its path will necessarily lead to heights of unimagined perfection*." There is, in fact, no "obligatory nature of the course of human civilization."[24] And yet, such a thing had been posited by politics in our time: "The communists believe that they have found the path to deliverance from our evils. . . . I have no concern with any economic criticisms of the communist system. I cannot enquire into whether the abolition of private property is expedient or advantageous. But I am able to recognize that the psychological premises on which the system is based are an untenable illusion."[25] Instead, Freud sees a state of permanent enmity between citizens and government with the latter inexorably becoming the rule of the few over the many. Why should that be so? It goes, after all, particularly against the grain of ideas of progress. Nearly every vision of perfection begins with benevolent rule. Freud, however, is convinced that aggressiveness in human nature runs too deep to be transfigured. Always with us, it necessarily becomes a disguised part of politics. When is aggression for the most part displayed? For the most part, surprisingly, in domestic affairs. "Aggression" in Freud may well lead to foreign wars—but it is primarily experienced in private lives. That is because the conflicts of private life are experienced daily, as are the pleasures of deciding them by force.

The central issue in Orwell is the internalization of fear within the individual mind. In *Nineteen Eighty-Four* even a monad cannot hold, and Parsons babbles in his sleep. In Freud, that is a state of mind actually called "bad conscience"—and it is instilled by "*external* authority." After this first stage, "comes the erection of an *internal* authority, and renunciation of instinct owing to fear of it—owing to fear of conscience. In this second situation bad intentions are equated with bad actions, and hence comes a sense of guilt and a need for punishment. The aggressiveness of conscience keeps up the aggressiveness of the authority."[26] This, I think, is the most logical context for O'Brien's claim that Winston and all other individuals will be filled up "with ourselves" (113). Citizens live in a constant state of induced anxiety. If—when—they can no longer renounce their instincts, they become incorrigibles like Winston and vanish as men.

Orwell depends on Freudian principles of human behavior governing individuals and groups. They are independent of regimes. While he was writing *Nineteen Eighty-Four*, he considered more than one kind of coercion.[27] In his review of the futurist novel *We* by Zamyatin he said, "what Zamyatin seems to be aiming at is not any particular country but the implied aims of industrial civilization."[28] Altered norms would lead to aberrations—a view shared by Lionel Trilling shortly after *Nineteen Eighty-Four* appeared. Trilling was one of the great Freudians, and he understood that "development" might be both idealistic and evil:

> The settled and reasoned opposition to Communism that Orwell expresses is not to be minimized, but he is not undertaking to give us the delusive comfort of moral superiority to an antagonist. He does not separate Russia from the general tendency of the world today. He is saying, indeed, something no less comprehensive than this: that Russia, with its idealistic social revolution now developed into a police state, is but the image of the impending future, and that the ultimate threat to human freedom may well come from a similar and even more massive development of the social idealism of our democratic culture. To many liberals, this idea will be incomprehensible. . . . [29]

In fact, the idea is by no means incomprehensible: in *The Republic* Plato argued that despotism proceeds from democracy.[30] The idea came to Orwell from the primary sources of political theory. He saw despotism as a natural outcome not because he was idiosyncratic but because he understood both texts and experience. One of his clearest statements about *Nine-*

teen Eighty-Four was published shortly after its publication: "Totalitarian ideas have taken root in the minds of intellectuals everywhere, and I have tried to draw these ideas out to their logical consequences."[31] That is why his novel of the future has so much to say about the past and why his own Grand Inquisitor takes such pride in his idea of progress.

Notes

INTRODUCTION

1. F. Scott Fitzgerald, "Winter Dreams," in *The Short Stories of F. Scott Fitzgerald*, ed. Matthew J. Bruccoli (New York: Charles Scribner's Sons, 1989), 217–36. Cited passage 226.
2. George Santayana, "Later Speculations," in *Character and Opinion in the United States* (1920; repr., Garden City: Doubleday Anchor Books, 1956), 86–102. Cited passages 99, 101. Emphasis added.
3. Marguerite Mooers Marshall, "F. Scott Fitzgerald, Novelist, Shocked by 'Younger Marrieds' and Prohibition," in *Conversations with F. Scott Fitzgerald*, ed. Matthew J. Bruccoli and Judith S. Baughman (Jackson: University Press of Mississippi, 2004), 26–29. Cited passage 27. For an important discussion of Fitzgerald's awareness of "philosophy" see Horst Kruse, "*The Great Gatsby:* A View from Kant's Window—Transatlantic Crosscurrents," *The F. Scott Fitzgerald Review* 2 (2003): 72–84, especially Notes, 81–82.
4. Sinclair Lewis, *Babbitt* (New York: Signet, 1980), 26.
5. F. Scott Fitzgerald, "Two For a Cent," in *Before Gatsby: The First Twenty-Six Stories*, ed. Matthew J. Bruccoli and Judith S. Baughman (Columbia: University of South Carolina Press, 2001), 409–22. Cited passage 409–11.
6. Robert S. Lynd and Helen Merrell Lynd, *Middletown* (San Diego: Harvest, 1957), 75. Originally published 1929.
7. Cited by Brian W. Aldiss in his introduction to H. G. Wells, *The War of the Worlds* (1898; repr., New York: Oxford University Press, 1995), xx. Discussion of the modern career of the Idea of Progress necessarily begins with Wells's *The Time Machine* of 1895. There are many citations of Wells in *F. Scott Fitzgerald*

on Authorship, ed. Matthew J. Bruccoli and Judith S. Baughman (Columbia: University of South Carolina Press, 1996) and in *F. Scott Fitzgerald: A Life in Letters,* ed. Matthew J. Bruccoli (New York: Touchstone, 1994). See "Such, Such Were the Joys," in *The Collected Essays, Journalism and Letters of George Orwell,* ed. Sonia Orwell and Ian Angus (New York: Harcourt, Brace & World, 1968), 4:330–69. Orwell writes that "Ian Hay, Thackeray, Kipling and H. G. Wells were the favourite authors of my boyhood" (344).

8. Herbert Spencer, *First Principles,* in H. G. Wells, *The Time Machine,* ed. Nicholas Ruddick (Ontario: Broadview, 2001), 192–93. Originally published 1862.

9. Bertrand Russell, "Adaptation: An Autobiographical Epitome," in *The Basic Writings of Bertrand Russell: 1903–59* (London: Routledge, 1992), 51–52.

10. Michael McGerr, *A Fierce Discontent: The Rise and Fall of the Progressive Movement in America 1870–1920* (New York: Free Press, 2003), 77–117; 118–46. There was a large agenda: "to reshape adult behavior. . . . improve the living conditions of workers . . . modernize the agrarian way of life" and "to reconstruct childhood." The eventual aim was "to remake Americans." Cited passage 79.

11. Russell, "Adaptation: An Autobiographical Epitome," 52.

12. Walter Lippmann, "Blind Spots and Their Value," in *Public Opinion* (1922; repr., New York: Free Press, 1997), 69–75. Cited passages 71–72.

13. See Ronald Berman, "Cultural Drift: A Context for Fiction," in *Fitzgerald, Hemingway, and the Twenties* (Tuscaloosa: University of Alabama Press, 2001), 11–27. See Fitzgerald's use of the term "drift" in the 1922 interview with Marguerite Mooers Marshall, "F. Scott Fitzgerald, Novelist," 27.

14. Lionel Trilling, "*The Bostonians,*" in *The Opposing Self* (New York: The Viking Press, 1955), 108–13.

15. Cited phrases are from "The Ice Palace," in *The Short Stories of F. Scott Fitzgerald,* 57, 58.

16. This citation is from *Tender Is the Night* in Milton R. Stern, "*Tender Is the Night* and American History," in *The Cambridge Companion to F. Scott Fitzgerald,* ed. Ruth Prigozy (Cambridge: Cambridge University Press, 2002), 95–117. Cited passage 110.

17. Ernest Hemingway, "Mr. and Mrs. Elliot," in *Ernest Hemingway: The Short Stories* (New York: Scribner, 1995), 161.

18. Walter Lippmann, *A Preface to Morals* (New York: Macmillan, 1929), 303.

19. Ibid., 304. Lippmann acknowledges many sources, which makes him useful as a compiler and reviewer of thought in the twenties. The cited phrase comes from Joseph Wood Krutch. It may be that Lippmann (223–24) had Hemingway in mind when he described a vanishing style of Americanism: the man who "holds himself to an ideal of conduct though it is inconvenient, unprofitable, or dangerous to do so." He does not "complain or ask for help in unavoidable or trifling calamities."

20. Lionel Trilling, "Hemingway and His Critics," in *Speaking of Literature and*

Society (New York: Harcourt Brace Jovanovich, 1980), 123–34. Cited passages 132, 133.

21. Dwight Macdonald, *Masscult & Midcult* (New York: Partisan Review and Random House, 1961), 56–57.

22. Isaiah Berlin, "The Divorce between the Sciences and the Humanities," in *Against the Current* (New York: Viking Press, 1980), 80–110, especially 80.

23. Berlin, "Vico and the Ideal of the Enlightenment," in *Against the Current,* 120–29, especially 123.

24. Hemingway's attack on the ideas in the *Forum* have their context. See Isaiah Berlin, "Marxism and the International in the Nineteenth Century," in *The Sense of Reality* (New York: Farrar, Straus and Giroux, 1996), 120–22.

25. Russell, "Philosophy in the Twentieth Century," in *Basic Writings,* 259–74. Cited passage 272.

26. McGerr, *A Fierce Discontent,* 236–37,

27. Russell, "General Ideas and Thought," in *The Analysis of Mind* (1921; repr., London: Routledge, 2002), 191.

28. Avrum Stroll, *Wittgenstein* (Oxford: Oneworld, 2002); *The Wittgenstein Reader,* ed. Anthony Kenny (Oxford: Blackwell, 1997).

29. *Ernest Hemingway: The Short Stories,* 260.

30. Ibid., 282.

31. Ernest Hemingway, *A Farewell to Arms* (1929; repr., New York: Charles Scribner's Sons, 1969), 179.

32. McGerr, *A Fierce Discontent,* 236.

33. Virginia Woolf, *Roger Fry: A Biography* (London: The Hogarth Press, 1940), 284–86.

34. See Theodore L. Gaillard Jr., "Hemingway's Debt to Cézanne: New Perspectives," in *Twentieth Century Literature* 45, no. 1 (Spring 1999): 65–78.

35. *The Politics of Aristotle,* ed. Ernest Barker (London: Oxford University Press, 1981), 244.

36. Ibid.

37. Sigmund Freud, *Civilization and Its Discontents,* ed. James Strachey (New York: W. W. Norton, 1989), 48–49.

CHAPTER 1

1. See Scott Donaldson, "Scott Fitzgerald's Romance with the South," in *Southern Literary Journal* 5 (1973): 3–17; C. Hugh Holman, "Fitzgerald's Changes on the Southern Belle: The Tarleton Trilogy," in *The Short Stories of F. Scott Fitzgerald: New Approaches in Criticism,* ed. Jackson R. Bryer (Madison: University of Wisconsin Press, 1982), 53–64; Heidi Kunz Bullock, "The Southern and the Satirical in 'The Last of the Belles'" in *New Essays on F. Scott Fitzgerald's Neglected Stories,* ed. Jackson R. Bryer (Columbia: University of Missouri Press, 1996), 130–37.

2. For indispensable coverage of the North-South opposition in Fitzgerald see Frederick Wegener, "The 'Two Civil Wars' of F. Scott Fitzgerald," in *F. Scott Fitzgerald in the Twenty-First Century*, ed. Jackson R. Bryer, Ruth Prigozy, and Milton R. Stern (Tuscaloosa: University of Alabama Press, 2003), 238–66. This essay cites a large number of passages in Fitzgerald that would otherwise be difficult to find.

3. Robert Nisbet, "Progress," in *Prejudices: A Philosophical Dictionary* (Cambridge, Mass.: Harvard University Press, 1982), 241.

4. Charles A. and Mary R. Beard, *The Rise of American Civilization* (New York: Macmillan, 1927), 800.

5. Nisbet, "Progress," 241.

6. See Ronald Berman, "'The Diamond' and the Declining West," in *Fitzgerald, Hemingway, and the Twenties* (Tuscaloosa and London: University of Alabama Press, 2001), 40–51.

7. See Ronald Berman, *The Great Gatsby and Modern Times* (Urbana: University of Illinois Press, 1994), 59–81; *The Great Gatsby and Fitzgerald's World of Ideas* (Tuscaloosa and London: The University of Alabama Press, 1997), 44–67.

8. F. Scott Fitzgerald, *The Great Gatsby*, ed. Matthew J. Bruccoli (1925; repr., Cambridge: Cambridge University Press, 1991), 131. Future references in parentheses in my text.

9. In H. L. Mencken, *Prejudices, Fourth Series* (New York: Knopf, 1924). Mencken's essay "Totentanz" is listed under "Places to Live" in *A Second Mencken Chrestomathy*, ed. Terry Teachout (New York: Alfred A. Knopf, 1995), 179–86. Cited passages 181, 185.

10. H. L. Mencken, "Metropolis," in *A Second Mencken Chrestomathy*, 186–91. Cited passage 189. See also Mencken's column from the *Baltimore Evening Sun* of July 26, 1926, reprinted in *The Impossible H. L. Mencken: A Selection of His Best Newspaper Stories*, ed. Marion Elizabeth Rodgers (New York: Anchor Books, 1991), 110–11. The assumption of Metropolis, as seen in *Vanity Fair* and the *New Yorker*, is that it personifies style. But Mencken states that the charm of the city "chiefly issues out of money," which makes style possible.

11. Mencken, "Totentanz," 181.

12. Bruccoli, *The Short Stories of F. Scott Fitzgerald*, 97. Future references in parentheses in my text.

13. *A Preface to Morals* (New York: Macmillan, 1929), 232–39.

14. Lewis Mumford, "The City," in *Civilization in the United States*, ed. Harold E. Stearns (London: Jonathan Cape, 1922), 3–20. Cited passage 9.

15. See note 7.

16. It was an artifact on Fitzgerald's mind. He wrote of Sherwood Anderson that "what he takes to be only an empty tomato can" may be one of those "lesser things" that have been "endowed . . . with significance." "Sherwood Anderson on the Marriage Question," in *F. Scott Fitzgerald on Authorship*, ed. Matthew J.

Bruccoli and Judith S. Baughman (Columbia: University of South Carolina Press, 1996), 83–85, especially 84.

17. Roland Marchand, *Advertising the American Dream* (Berkeley: University of California Press, 1986), 223. Images in the public realm rivaled categorical thought: "A well-placed radiant beam of light from a mysterious heavenly source might create a virtual halo around the advertised object without provoking the reader into outrage at the advertiser's presumption." These techniques of silence suggested patriotism, religion, and progress through a sequence of technological improvement. (236–38).

18. Cited by Terry Teachout, *The Skeptic: A Life of H. L. Mencken* (New York: HarperCollins, 2002), 244. From "Little White Girl," *Scribner's,* April 1934, 78.

19. Alice Hall Petry, *Fitzgerald's Craft of Short Fiction* (Tuscaloosa and London: University of Alabama Press, 1989), 43.

20. See Fred Hobson, *Serpent in Eden: H. L. Mencken and the South* (Baton Rouge: Louisiana State University Press, 1978), 4: "It was in the field of *belles lettres* that Mencken's efforts were most noticeable. His notorious essay, the "Sahara," had been directed in particular at the literary poverty of the postbellum South."

21. Santayana, "Materialism and Idealism in American Life," in *Character and Opinion in the United States,* 109.

22. *Santayana on America,* ed. Richard Colton Lyon (New York: Harcourt, Brace & World, 1968), 207. From *The Idler and His Works* in 1957, but a continuation of Santayana's observations on national character since the 1900s. Emphasis added.

23. Stanley Brodwin, "F. Scott Fitzgerald and Willa Cather," in *F. Scott Fitzgerald in the Twenty-First Century,* 173–89. Cited passage 183.

24. C. Hugh Holman, "Fitzgerald's Changes on the Southern Belle," 55.

25. *The Golden Moment: The Novels of F. Scott Fitzgerald* (Urbana: University of Illinois Press, 1971), 253.

26. "Preface," *Civilization in the United States,* vii.

27. *William Faulkner: Toward Yoknapatawpha and Beyond* (New Haven: Yale University Press, 1979), 272. Frederick Wegener cites Fitzgerald on the personification of "the brilliant success of the North" and "the golden beauty of the South," *F. Scott Fitzgerald in the Twenty-First Century,* 252.

28. John O'Donnell, "Fitzgerald Condemns St. Paul Flappers: 'Unattractive, Selfish, Graceless,' Are Adjectives Applied to Middle West Girls," in *Conversations with F. Scott Fitzgerald,* 30–31. Cited passage 31. Originally published in the *St. Paul Daily News,* sec. 1, April 16, 1922.

29. F. Wilson, "F. Scott Fitzgerald Says: 'All Women Over Thirty-Five Should Be Murdered,'" in *Conversations with F. Scott Fitzgerald,* 55–59. Cited passage 57. Originally published in the *Metropolitan Magazine* 58 (November 1923): 34, 75–76.

30. *The Price Was High: The Last Uncollected Stories of F. Scott Fitzgerald,* ed.

Matthew J. Bruccoli (New York: Harvest, 1979), 35. Future references in parentheses in my text.

31. *The Complete Works of Shakespeare,* ed. David Bevington (New York: Harper-Collins, 1992), 185.

32. Sigmund Freud, *Writings on Art and Literature,* ed. Werner Hamacher and David E. Wellbury (Stanford: Stanford University Press, 1997), 109–21. The essay was translated into English in Freud's *Complete Psychological Works* of 1913.

33. Ibid., 120

34. Ibid., 119.

35. Ibid., 120

36. Ibid., 118.

CHAPTER 2

1. Lippmann, *A Preface to Morals,* 303, 304.

2. Van Wyck Brooks, *America's Coming-Of-Age* (Garden City: Doubleday Anchor Books, 1958), 77. Brooks likened the national mind to the Sargasso Sea (76–88), which is broad but completely formless.

3. Donald Ogden Stewart, *A Parody Outline of History* (New York: G. H. Doran, 1921), title page.

4. See Bickford Sylvester, "Hemingway's Italian *Waste Land:* The Complex Unity of 'Out of Season,'" in *Hemingway's Neglected Short Fiction: New Perspectives,* ed. Susan F. Beegel (Ann Arbor: UMI Research Press, 1989), 75–98, especially 76.

5. Thomas Strychacz, "*In Our Time,* Out of Season," in *The Cambridge Companion to Hemingway,* ed. Scott Donaldson (Cambridge: Cambridge University Press, 1996), 55–86. Cited passage 55.

6. Donald Davidson, "Knowing One's Own Mind," in *Subjective, Intersubjective, Objective* (Oxford: Clarendon Press, 2001), 15. Hemingway's constant use of the phrase may be modeled on the practice of Gertrude Stein, who believed that meanings accumulate through restatement. Her biographer, James R. Mellow, argues that there was a three-sided connection between the technique of Cézanne, Stein's derivations from that technique, and her advice to Hemingway about both painting and writing. Stein thought that the work of Cézanne involved the repetition of identical brush strokes that were equivalent to "reiterative phrases." She translated from painting to writing an idea of "repeated strokes," the fundamental unit being "one stroke" subject to "infinitely patient repetition." In other words, Hemingway was invited not only to admire Cézanne but to think of adapting his style by a kind of equivalent multiplication. Mellow likens the process to brickwork. The notion is that of building a structure that remains unique although composed of bricks identical to those used in other structures. See James R. Mellow, *Hemingway: A Life Without Consequences* (Boston: Houghton Mifflin, 1992), 151.

7. H. L. Mencken, "American and English," in *The American Language* (New York: Alfred A. Knopf, 2000), 292–94. Earlier editions published in 1919, 1921, 1923, and 1936.

8. Hemingway, *The Short Stories* (New York: Simon & Schuster, 1995), 179. Future references in parentheses in my text.

9. Hemingway, *The Sun Also Rises* (1926; repr., New York: Charles Scribner's Sons, 1970), 52. Future references in parentheses in my text.

10. Alfred B. Kuttner, "Nerves," in *Civilization in the United States*, 427–42. Cited passages 427.

11. H. L. Mencken, *The American Language*, 293–94.

12. Isaiah Berlin, "Rousseau," in *Freedom and Its Betrayal*, ed. Henry Hardy (Princeton: Princeton University Press, 2002), 31.

13. For analysis of the story's language see Scott Donaldson, "Preparing for the End: Hemingway's Revisions of 'A Canary for One,'" in *New Critical Approaches to the Short Stories of Ernest Hemingway*, ed. Jackson J. Benson (Durham: Duke University Press, 1990), 229–37, especially 233–34, which describe revisions intended to emphasize "the American lady's unreliability."

14. Donald Davidson, *Subjective, Intersubjective, Objective*, 53.

15. Ibid., 67.

16. Ibid., 4.

17. Ibid., 210.

18. George Santayana, "Love," in *The Life of Reason* (1905; repr., New York: Charles Scribner's Sons, 1919), 2:17.

19. *The Only Thing That Counts: The Ernest Hemingway-Maxwell Perkins Correspondence 1925–47*, ed. Matthew J. Bruccoli and Robert W. Trogden (Columbia: University of South Carolina Press, 1996), 151.

20. Marilyn Elkins, "The Fashion of *Machismo*," in *A Historical Guide to Ernest Hemingway*, ed. Linda Wagner-Martin (New York: Oxford University Press, 2000), 104.

21. When Fitzgerald edited the manuscript of *A Farewell to Arms* in the spring of 1929 he pointed out that "Catherine is too glib, talks too much physically. In cutting their conversations cut some of her speeches rather than his." Hemingway, he thought, had an uncritical attitude about her. In Matthew J. Bruccoli, *Some Sort of Epic Grandeur* (Columbia: University of South Carolina Press, 2002), 273. Mellow writes in *Hemingway: A Life Without Consequences*, 84, "in a sentimental poem in praise of his friend, Hemingway recalled their heavy drinking sessions and their talk, talk, talk of the empire, the separate trades of soldiering and writing, the necessity of money, overdrafts, and how to handle tailors."

22. See Hemingway's "Shootism Versus Sport: The Second Tanganyika Letter," in *By-Line: Ernest Hemingway*, ed. William White (1935; repr., New York: Touchstone, 1998), 162–66.

23. Fernand Braudel, "Superfluity and Sufficiency," in *The Structures of Everyday Life* (New York: Harper & Row, 1981), 266–333. Cited passage 323.

24. Ibid., 333. In 1929, Edmund Wilson saw the signs of "a tighter, compacter, and more downright civilization" in English artifacts. He derived some of these ideas from the philosophy of Alfred North Whitehead, who had recently posited the relationship between different minds focused on common objects. See Ronald Berman, "Edmund Wilson and Alfred North Whitehead," in *Fitzgerald-Wilson-Hemingway* (Tuscaloosa: University of Alabama Press, 2003), 53–55.

25. The phrase is from the conclusion of Ben Jonson's "To Penshurst."

26. This story appeared in the *Little Review* of 1926 in response to the editor Jane Heap's invitation to write about "travesties" of "art, originality, or any psychological complication." See Michael Reynolds, *Hemingway: The Paris Years* (Oxford: Basil Blackwell, 1990), 266–67. Edmund Wilson praised the story, which was cleaned up considerably before appearing in *Men Without Women*. See Mellow, *Hemingway: A Life Without Consequences*, 352–53.

27. See George Monteiro, "The Writer on Vocation: Hemingway's 'Banal Story,'" in Beegel, *Hemingway's Neglected Short Fiction*, 141–47. Cited passage 147.

28. H. L. Mencken probably had the last word on that issue: how could one possibly elicit uniformity from a nation made up of "Knights of Pythias, Presbyterians, Ph.D.'s, Prohibitionists, readers of the *Saturday Evening Post*, admirers of Massenet, sitters on committees, weepers at Chatauquas, wearers of badges, honest householders, children of God. . . . " From "Diagnosis of Our Cultural Malaise," in *H. L. Mencken's Smart Set Criticism*, ed. William H. Nolte (Washington: Gateway, 1987), 2.

29. See the first-rate coverage of the *Forum* in the twenties by Wayne Kvam, "Hemingway's 'Banal Story,'" in *New Critical Approaches to the Short Stories of Ernest Hemingway*, 215–23. Cited passage 217. Mencken's phrase for the lowering of mind was "joining the mob against sense." In "Diagnosis of Our Cultural Malaise," 5.

30. Maury Klein, *Rainbow's End: The Crash of 1929* (New York: Oxford University Press, 2001), 137. Klein adds that "Coolidge had called the factory a temple and work a form of worship, but business itself was fast becoming the new religion." He cites Arthur M. Schlesinger on "the metaphysics of optimism," which gave a moral basis to supporting the rising stock market (103).

31. See "Tractatus Logico-Philosophicus," in *The Wittgenstein Reader*, ed. Anthony Kenny (Oxford: Blackwell, 1997), 30–31. Originally published 1922.

32. Kvam, "Hemingway's 'Banal Story,'" 217.

33. See "Tractatus Logico-Philosophicus," 31.

34. Lippmann, *A Preface to Morals*, 110.

35. Isaiah Berlin, *The Hedgehog and the Fox* (New York: Simon and Schuster, 1953), 37. Emphasis added.

36. Isaiah Berlin, "The Originality of Machiavelli," in *Against the Current* (New York: Viking, 1980). 25–79. Cited passage 41.

37. Isaiah Berlin, "The Counter-Enlightenment," in *Against the Current,* 1–24.

38. See the discussion of "critical incomprehension" by Robert E. Gajdusek, "Hemingway and Joyce: A Study in Debt and Payment," in *Hemingway in His Own Country* (Notre Dame, Indiana: University of Notre Dame Press, 2002), 9–56. Cited phrase 19.

39. Kvam, "Hemingway's 'Banal Story,'" 217.

40. Gajdusek, "Hemingway and Joyce," 12.

41. *The Short Stories,* 189, 207, 265–66; *Death in the Afternoon* (1932; repr., New York: Charles Scribner's Sons, 1960), 82–83, 198.

42. *The Only Thing That Counts,* 92.

43. Ibid., 100

44. William James, "Concerning Fechner," in *William James: Writings 1902–1910,* ed. Bruce Kuklick (New York: Literary Classics of the United States, 1987), 709.

45. See Santayana, "Materialism and Idealism in American Life," *Character and Opinion in the United States,* 102–18. "What exists seems . . . irrational accidents and bad habits, and they [the majority of minds] want the future to be based on reason" (109).

CHAPTER 3

1. Santayana, "Materialism and Idealism in American Life," 102–18. Cited passage 115.

2. Charles A. and Mary R. Beard, *The Rise of American Civilization,* (New York: Macmillan, 1927), 2:758–62, 781–82, 798. See Maury Klein, *Rainbow's End: The Crash of 1929* (New York: Oxford University Press, 2001), 84: "Americans loved numbers. A quantitative people who measured rather than evaluated greatness, they doted on figures of every kind, whether income or output, batting averages or stock prices, election returns or sizes of fortunes. Their sense of the present and vision of the future began with the assumption that more was better."

3. Fitzgerald, *The Great Gatsby,* 70–71.

4. Santayana, "Materialism and Idealism in American Life," 106–13.

5. Fitzgerald, *This Side of Paradise,* ed. James L. W. West III (1920; repr., Cambridge: Cambridge University Press, 1995), 185.

6. Stephen Kern, *The Culture of Time and Space 1880–1918* (Cambridge, Mass.: Harvard University Press, 1983), 29. See J. Gerald Kennedy's discussion of *Tender Is the Night,* which refers to Kern, to Bergson on "the distinction between public time and inner, subjective time," and to Proust's "explorations of the psychological experience of time." In *Imagining Paris* (New Haven: Yale University Press, 1993), 185–219. Cited passages 187.

7. Kern, *Culture of Time and Space*, 63.

8. See William R. Everdell, "Discontinuous Epilogues," in *The First Moderns* (Chicago: University of Chicago Press, 1998), 348–49.

9. H. G. Wells, *The Outline of History* (New York: Macmillan, 1921), 1098–1100.

10. Charles A. and Mary R. Beard, *The Rise of American Civilization*, 2:800.

11. Van Wyck Brooks, "The Literary Life," and Lewis Mumford, "The City," in *Civilization in the United States*, 3–20, 179–198.

12. Lippmann, *Public Opinion*, 89 (see introduction, n. 12). Emphasis added. See the discussion of time by Edward Gillin in "Princeton, Pragmatism, and Fitzgerald's Sentimental Journey," in *F. Scott Fitzgerald in the Twenty-First Century*, 38–53.

13. Ibid., 90.

14. See Kern, *The Culture of Time and Space 1880–1918*, 83–5. Kern (330–31) cites William James's *Principles of Psychology*, Royce's *The World and the Individual*, and *Selected Writings of Gertrude Stein*, ed. F. W. Dupee.

15. Bertrand Russell, *The Analysis of Mind* (1921; repr., London: Routledge, 2002), 144–46.

16. Lippmann, *Public Opinion*, 90.

17. According to the *Oxford English Dictionary*, "recording and arranging events in the order of time."

18. F. Scott Fitzgerald, "Echoes of the Jazz Age," in *The Crack-Up*, ed. Edmund Wilson (New York: New Directions, 1956), 13–22. Future references in parentheses in my text.

19. Fitzgerald, *The Great Gatsby*, 49, 68, 134–35.

20. Fitzgerald, "Dalyrimple Goes Wrong," in *Before Gatsby*, 59–72 (see introduction, n. 5). Cited passage 62.

21. Ibid., 399.

22. Fitzgerald, *The Stories of F. Scott Fitzgerald*, ed. Malcolm Cowley (New York: Charles Scribner's Sons, 1951), 309.

23. Ibid., 44.

24. John Dewey, "The Lost Individual," in *The Philosophy of John Dewey*, ed. John J. McDermott (Chicago: University of Chicago Press, 1981), 605–7.

25. See Ronald Berman, *The Great Gatsby and Fitzgerald's World of Ideas* (Tuscaloosa: University of Alabama Press, 1997), 63–67.

26. F. Scott Fitzgerald, "Basil And Cleopatra," in *The Short Stories of F. Scott Fitzgerald*, 431–48. Cited passage 441.

27. Peter Conrad, "Interrogating the Universe," in *Modern Times, Modern Places* (New York: Alfred A. Knopf, 1999), 61.

28. Ibid., 78–79.

29. Michael Reynolds, *The Sun Also Rises: A Novel of the Twenties* (Boston: Twayne Publishers, 1988), 90. See the extended discussion of Hemingway and Einstein in Michael Reynolds, "'Homage to Switzerland': Einstein's Train Stops at Hem-

ingway's Station," in *Hemingway's Neglected Short Fiction: New Perspectives,* 255–62.

30. Everdell, *The First Moderns,* 236.

31. Edmund Wilson, "A. N. Whitehead: Physicist and Prophet," in *From the Uncollected Edmund Wilson,* ed. Janet Groth and David Castronovo (Athens, Ohio: Ohio University Press, 1995), 56–72. Cited passage 67.

32. Edmund Wilson, "Marcel Proust," in *Axel's Castle* (1931; repr., New York: Charles Scribner's Sons, 1954), 132–90. Cited passage 162–63.

33. Ibid., 297–98.

34. F. Scott Fitzgerald, "A Short Trip Home," in *The Short Stories of F. Scott Fitzgerald,* 372–89. Cited passage 386.

35. Leonard Shlain, *Art and Physics* (New York: Perennial, 1991), 134.

36. Alfred North Whitehead, "Science and the Modern World," in *Alfred North Whitehead: An Anthology,* ed. F. S. C. Northrop and Mason W. Gross (New York: Macmillan, 1953), 452.

37. Fitzgerald, *The Great Gatsby,* 54.

38. Ibid., 119. See the lengthy account of Einstein's thought about a moving train and its station in Shlain, *Art and Physics,* 120–30.

39. Fitzgerald, *The Great Gatsby,* 126.

40. A. S. Eddington, "Relativity," in *Space, Time, and Gravitation: An Outline of the General Relativity Theory* (Cambridge: Cambridge University Press, 1920), 23–32.

41. Ibid., 23–24.

42. Alfred North Whitehead's "Adventures of Ideas" (1933) argues that self-examination is best understood by poetry. He states that "an appeal to literature, to common language, to common practice" provides "a perspective apprehension of the world" superior to epistemology. In *Alfred North Whitehead: An Anthology,* 846–47.

43. Whitehead, "Science and the Modern World," 452.

44. William James, "On the Notion of Reality as Changing," in *The Writings of William James,* ed. John J. McDermott (Chicago: University of Chicago Press, 1977), 301–4. Cited passages 303. Emphasis added.

45. Ruth Prigozy has reminded me that "Babylon Revisited" is probably the most important of Fitzgerald's writings on time. Its complex structure covers the perceptions of seven years within a bewildering scale of smaller units of experience.

CHAPTER 4

1. Hemingway, *A Farewell to Arms,* 8. The text refers to whorehouses in Naples. As Bill Gorton says in *The Sun Also Rises,* "give them Irony. . . . Just a little irony. . . . They're mad about it in New York." (114). Future references to *The Sun Also Rises* in parentheses in my text.

2. Cited by David Gilmour, *The Long Recessional: The Imperial Life of Rudyard Kipling* (New York: Farrar, Straus and Giroux, 2002), 108. See Edmund Wilson, "The Kipling That Nobody Read," in *The Wound and the Bow* (New York: Oxford, 1965), 123–28.

3. There are exceptions: H. L. Mencken wrote a poem about Kipling in 1899 with the line, "forget politics and go back to Mandalay." Cited by Teachout, *The Skeptic: A Life of H. L. Mencken*, 54 (see chap. 1, n. 18).

4. Marjorie Perloff, *Wittgenstein's Ladder* (Chicago: University of Chicago Press, 1996), 1, 2. The first passage is from *Notes on Logic* (1913) and the second from the *Tractatus* (1922).

5. Ernest Hemingway, "Soldier's Home," in *The Short Stories*, 147–48.

6. See the notorious interview with Lillian Ross, "How Do You Like It Now, Gentlemen?", in *Hemingway: A Collection of Critical Essays*, ed. Robert P. Weeks (Englewood Cliffs: Prentice-Hall, 1962), 17–39. Hemingway quoted the boxer Jack Britton: "One time, I asked Jack, speaking of a fight with Benny Leonard, 'How did you handle Benny so easy, Jack?' 'Ernie,' he said, 'Benny is an awfully smart boxer. All the time he's boxing, he's thinking. All the time he was thinking, I was hitting him'" (28).

7. Hemingway, "The Undefeated," in *The Short Stories*, 260.

8. Bertrand Russell, "General Ideas and Thought," 191 (see introduction, n. 27).

9. Avrum Stroll, *Wittgenstein*, 91–2 (see introduction, n. 28).

10. Edmund Wilson, "Gilbert Seldes and the Popular Arts," in *The Shores of Light* (New York: Farrar, Straus and Young, 1952), 156–64. See Berman, *Fitzgerald, Hemingway, and the Twenties*, 67–70.

11. Wilson, "A. N. Whitehead: Physicist and Prophet," 67.

12. Edmund Wilson to Maxwell Perkins, n.d. (probably September 1928), in *Letters on Literature and Politics*, ed. Elena Wilson (New York: Farrar, Straus and Giroux, 1977), 149–51.

13. Edmund Wilson, *The Twenties*, ed. Leon Edel (New York: Farrar, Straus and Giroux, 1975), 312.

14. Wilson, *Axel's Castle*, 91, 296–97.

15. Ludwig Wittgenstein, *The Wittgenstein Reader*, ed. Anthony Kenny (Oxford: Blackwell, 1997), 111–17.

16. Hemingway, "Soldier's Home," in *The Short Stories*, 151–52.

17. Sigmund Freud, "On the Mechanism of Paranoia," in *General Psychological Theory*, ed. Philip Rieff (New York: Collier, 1963), 35.

18. See Wittgenstein, *Tractatus Logico-Philosophicus*, ed. Bertrand Russell (1922; repr., Mineola, N.Y.: Dover, 1999), 53.

19. Hemingway, "The Killers," *The Short Stories*, 280–89.

20. Mencken, "The Commonwealth of Morons" in *A Second Mencken Chrestomathy*, 9. From H. L. Mencken, *Prejudices: Third Series* (New York: Knopf, 1922). See Berman, *Fitzgerald, Hemingway, and the Twenties*, 76–7.

21. Hemingway, "Monologue to the Maestro; A High Seas Letter," in *By-Line: Ernest Hemingway*, 219.

22. Hemingway, *The Short Stories*, 363, 367.

23. Hemingway, *A Farewell to Arms*, 51.

24. Russell, *The Analysis of Mind*, 9.

25. Hemingway, *Death in the Afternoon*, 1–2.

26. Davidson, *Subjective, Intersubjective, Objective*, 52.

27. Stroll, *Wittgenstein*, 77–8.

28. Ibid., 81.

29. Hemingway, *Death in the Afternoon*, 189.

30. Hemingway, "The Undefeated," in *The Short Stories*, 245–56.

31. Carlos Baker, *Ernest Hemingway: A Life Story* (New York: Charles Scribner's Sons, 1969), 90–91.

32. Claude Caswell, "City of Brothelly Love: The Influence of Paris and Prostitution on Hemingway's Fiction," in *French Connections: Hemingway and Fitzgerald Abroad*, ed. J. Gerald Kennedy and Jackson R. Bryer (New York: St. Martin's Press, 1999), 75–100. See especially 95–97. I don't agree that Hemingway was principally "a seer, a watcher, a wandering camera—a voyeur." That underestimates the process of perception, which is not simply a stance or technique. See the chapter "Reality's Thickness" in Berman, *Fitzgerald-Wilson-Hemingway*, 58–74.

33. Scott Donaldson, "The Averted Gaze in Hemingway's Fiction," *Sewanee Review* 3 (Winter 2003): 128–51. Cited passage 151. Emphasis added.

34. Ibid., 260.

35. Stroll, *Wittgenstein*, 79–80.

36. Ibid., 80.

37. Hemingway, *A Farewell to Arms*, 327.

38. John Dewey, "Experience and Thinking," in *The Philosophy of John Dewey*, 500–01. Published originally in *Democracy and Education* (1916). It would be a great mistake to underestimate the reputation or abilities of John Dewey. See Richard Rorty, "The Invisible Philosopher," *New York Times Book Review*, March 9, 2003, 14: "The most influential philosophers of the 20th century were John Dewey, Martin Heidegger, Bertrand Russell, and Ludwig Wittgenstein. . . . [Dewey was] our country's most useful public intellectual."

39. Dewey, "Experience and Thinking," in *The Philosophy of John Dewey*, 501–02.

40. Ibid., 503.

41. Ibid., 504.

42. Cited by Edward F. Stanton, *Hemingway and Spain* (Seattle: University of Washington Press, 1989), 208.

43. Ibid., 505.

44. Hemingway, *A Farewell to Arms*, 179.

CHAPTER 5

1. See Pavel Machotka, *Cézanne: Landscape into Art* (New Haven: Yale University Press, 1996). This collection of plates and of photographs of their sites is invaluable for Hemingway scholars.

2. Cited by Diane Kelder in *The Great Book of French Impressionism* (New York: Cross River Press, 1980), 386. From Meyer Schapiro, *Cézanne* (New York: H. N. Abrams, 1952), 10.

3. Meyly Chin Hagemman, "Hemingway's Secret: Visual to Verbal Art," *Journal of Modern Literature* 7, no. 1 (February 1979): 87–112. Cited passage 108. See Erik Nakjavani, "Repetition as Design and Intention: Hemingway's 'Homage to Switzerland,'" in *Hemingway's Neglected Short Fiction*, 263–82. For an overview see J. Hillis Miller, *Fiction and Repetition* (Cambridge: Harvard University Press, 1982).

4. Kenneth G. Johnston, "Hemingway and Cézanne: Doing the Country," *American Literature* 56, no. 1 (March 1984): 28–37. Cited passage 29–30. This article has the deleted lines from "Big Two-Hearted River" about Nick Adams trying to imitate Paul Cézanne (31). Beginning with this article, I have cited many titles of Cézanne. These titles, whether in English or French, exist in variant forms. Whenever a title is cited, it is in the form used by the source. Different publications are cited because of variations in the reproduction (color, size, detail, quality) of paintings or drawings.

5. Emily Stipes Watts, *Ernest Hemingway and the Arts* (Urbana: University of Illinois Press, 1971), 29–50. Cited passage 44.

6. Ibid.

7. Ross, "How Do You Like It Now, Gentlemen?" in *Hemingway: A Collection of Critical Essays*, 17–39. Cited passage 36. See Gaillard Jr., "Hemingway's Debt to Cézanne," 65–78 (see introduction, n. 34).

8. See Watts, *Ernest Hemingway and the Arts*, 146–49.

9. Lionello Venturi, *Cézanne* (New York: Rizzoli, 1978); *Cézanne: The Late Work*, ed. William Rubin (New York: The Museum of Modern Art, 1977); John Rewald, *The Paintings of Paul Cézanne: A Catalogue Raisonné*, 2 vols. (New York: Harry N. Abrams, 1996).

10. F. Novotny, "The Late Landscape Paintings," in *Cézanne: The Late Work*, 107–11. Cited passages 110–11.

11. Geneviève Monnier, "The Late Watercolors," in *Cézanne: The Late Work*, 113–18. Cited passage 116.

12. Hemingway, *The Short Stories*, 115. Future references to the stories in parentheses in my text.

13. The *OED* entry is under *naturalistic*.

14. *Cézanne: The Late Work*, 400, 414.

15. Ibid., 412; *Cézanne: Landscape into Art*, 56–57.

16. Cited by Meyer Schapiro, *Paul Cézanne,* 2nd ed. (New York: Harry N. Abrams, 1962), 108. Schapiro's allusion is to "The Great Pine."

17. Carlos Baker, *Hemingway: The Writer as Artist* (Princeton: Princeton University Press, 1973), 352.

18. Ernest Hemingway, *A Moveable Feast* (New York: Charles Scribner's Sons, 1964), 7, 13.

19. Cited in the *Cézanne* entry in *The Oxford Companion to Art,* ed. Harold Osborne (Oxford: Clarendon Press, 1970), 215–16. See Machotka on the essential rightness of Roger Fry's judgment, *Cézanne: Landscape into Art,* xiii, 1–7.

20. Jakob Rosenberg states that Fry's critical understanding of Cézanne has not been surpassed. See *On Quality in Art* (Princeton: Princeton University Press, 1967), 101. For a full treatment of Fry's standing see Alfred Werner's introduction to Fry's *Cézanne: A Study of His Development* (1927; repr., New York: Farrar, Straus and Giroux, 1970), i–xiii.

21. Woolf, *Roger Fry: A Biography,* 149–81 (see introduction, n. 33). Cited passages 177–78.

22. Ibid., 284–86.

23. Fry, *Cézanne: A Study of His Development,* 78–79.

24. Machotka, *Cézanne: Landscape into Art,* 1–2.

25. Robert W. Lewis, "Hemingway's Sense of Place," in *Hemingway in Our Time,* ed. Richard Astro and Jackson J. Benson (Corvallis: Oregon University Press, 1974), 113–43. Cited passages 119–21.

26. Ibid., 143.

27. The Hemingway scene should be compared to Cézanne's *Route tournante en haut du Chemin des Lauves,* which is reproduced in Machotka, *Cézanne: Landscape into Art,* 114. It is especially helpful to see the black-and-white photograph taken in 1904. I have used the term "Impressionism" as Hemingway used it, as a kind of shorthand including post-Impressionism.

28. Novotny, "The Late Landscape Paintings," 111.

29. Hemingway, *The Sun Also Rises,* 93. Future references to this novel in parentheses in my text.

30. Armand Guillaumin, "The Outskirts of Paris," in *Impressionism: A Centenary Exhibition* (Paris: The Metropolitan Museum of Art, 1974), 108–9.

31. Schapiro, *Paul Cézanne,* 118. See Hemingway's letter "To Henry Strater, Nordquist Ranch, 14 October 1932," in *Ernest Hemingway: Selected Letters,* ed. Carlos Baker (New York: Charles Scribner's Sons, 1981), 369: "A man can be a hell of a serious artist and not have to make his living by it—see Flaubert, Cézanne and Co." The remark is enigmatic without knowing the conclusion of Roger Fry's *Cézanne: A Study of His Development.* According to Fry, novelist and painter were connected by romanticism, technique, "infinitely laborious" reconstruction of their work—and by their financial independence, which allowed them to do their work without kowtowing to critics. (87–88). Michael

Reynolds writes in *Hemingway: The Paris Years* (Oxford: Blackwell, 1990) that Flaubert's *Sentimental Education* was on the "list of required reading" Ezra Pound gave to Hemingway in winter 1921–22 and that Gertrude Stein often recommended Cézanne in spring 1922. At that time, Hemingway "listened and looked and went to the Luxembourg Musée to see more Cézannes, landscapes and bathers." (29–30, 40).

32. Kelder, *The Great Book of French Impressionism*, 390–91.

33. See Meyer Schapiro's discussion of "Turning Road at Montgeroult," in *Paul Cézanne*, 112.

34. Isaiah Berlin, *The Sense of Reality* (New York: Farrar, Straus and Giroux, 1996), 170.

35. Ibid., 173–74.

36. Hans-Johann Glock, "Wittgenstein and Reason," in *Wittgenstein: Biography and Philosophy*, ed. James C. Klagge (Cambridge: Cambridge University Press, 2001), 195–220. Cited passage 207. Klagge cites M. Drury, "Some Notes on Conversations with Wittgenstein," in *Recollections of Wittgenstein*, ed. R. Rhees (Oxford: Oxford University Press, 1984).

37. Margaret Anne Doody, *The True Story of the Novel* (New Brunswick: Rutgers University Press, 1997), 321: a number of modern novels begin "on a shore, strand, bank, or marsh," including those of Conrad, Flaubert, Joyce, and Woolf.

38. Hemingway, *The Sun Also Rises*, 88–108.

39. Machotka, *Cézanne: Landscape into Art*, 113–19. Cited passage 119.

40. See Rewald, *The Paintings of Paul Cézanne*, 1:545. Rewald points out that these roads, which were "all over the region of Aix," became part of the paintings of Mont Sainte-Victoire.

41. Rewald, "The Last Motifs at Aix," in *Cézanne: the Late Work*, 104.

42. Rewald, *The Paintings of Paul Cézanne* 1:539.

43. Ibid., 1:546. Rewald alludes in his elaborate notes to E. H. Gombrich, Max Raphael, Lionello Venturi, and other historians of art. My discussion of the Mont Sainte-Victoire paintings relies on these citations. Cited passages 539, 545–47. Note especially Rewald's account of the reliability of the Gasquet interview.

44. Schapiro, *Paul Cézanne*, 74.

45. Ibid., 80.

CHAPTER 6

1. Czeslaw Milosz, *The Captive Mind*, cited in *George Orwell: The Critical Heritage*, ed. Jeffrey Meyers (1953; repr., London: Routledge & Kegan Paul, 1975), 286.

2. See Mark Falcoff, "Watching Christopher Hitchens," *Commentary*, January 2003, 41–4. See especially 43: Are Orwell's values "respected and honored in such post-imperialist, post-colonial nirvanas as Vietnam, Cambodia, Cuba,

Syria, Algeria? . . . How does the fate of their people today compare with the earlier periods of European administration?" Hitchens's *Why Orwell Matters* (New York: Basic Books, 2002) covers the politics of Orwell and of his critics. See also *George Orwell,* ed. Graham Holderness, Bryan Loughrey, and Nahem Yousaf (New York: St. Martin's Press, 1998), especially the essays of Richard Rorty, "The Last Intellectual in Europe" (139–61) and John Rodden, "On the Political Sociology of Intellectuals: George Orwell and the London Left Intelligentsia" (161–81).

3. Freud, *Civilization and Its Discontents,* 81–82 (see introduction, n. 37).

4. Orwell, "Such, Such Were the Joys," *The Collected Essays, Journalism and Letters of George Orwell,* 4:336 (see introduction, n. 7).

5. Ibid., 338.

6. *The Politics of Aristotle,* 227 (see introduction, n. 35). Future citations in parentheses in my text. This standard edition was first published in 1946, just as Orwell began thinking about his novel of the future. The preface (iv) points out that Aristotle was an important source of ideas for mid-twentieth century intellectuals.

7. Orwell may have been influenced by the discussion of spies and delators under Tiberius. Household spies reported Nero Caesar whether he "spoke or remained silent. . . . whether he slept, or lay awake, or sighed." Tacitus, *The Annals of Imperial Rome,* trans. Michael Grant (Harmondsworth, UK: Penguin, 1964), 183.

8. George Orwell, *Nineteen Eighty-Four,* ed. Irving Howe (1949; repr., New York: Harcourt, Brace & World, 1963), 119. Future citations in parentheses in my text.

9. Herodotus, *The Persian Wars,* trans. George Rawlinson (New York: Modern Library, 1942), 417.

10. See Lionel Trilling, "Freud's Last Book," in *A Gathering of Fugitives* (Boston: Beacon Press, 1956), 56–59. Trilling believes that although the "death instinct" may not have psychoanalytic value, it decidedly does have conceptual value, underlying the idea of tragic reality.

11. Hannah Arendt, *The Origins of Totalitarianism* (Cleveland: Meridian, 1962), 433.

12. Ibid., 426.

13. Freud, *Civilization and Its Discontents,* 82. See Trilling, "Freud's Last Book," 57: "If we look for an analogue to Freud's vision of life, we find it, I think, in certain great literary minds."

14. Freud, *Civilization and Its Discontents,* 73.

15. Sigmund Freud, *The Future Of An Illusion,* ed. James Strachey (New York: W. W. Norton, 1961), 5–9.

16. Ibid., 39.

17. Freud, *Civilization and Its Discontents,* 79, 94–112.

18. Isaiah Berlin, *Against the Current* (New York: Viking, 1980), 66–67.

19. Robert Graves, *The Greek Myths* (Baltimore: Penguin, 1966), 1:27, 31–5.

20. *The Republic of Plato,* ed. Francis MacDonald Cornford (New York: Oxford University Press, 1965) 209 (vi. 500), 298 (ix. 572).
21. From Shakespeare, *Troilus and Cressida,* act 1, scene 3, 114–22.
22. Freud, *Civilization and Its Discontents,* 80.
23. Ibid., 81–82.
24. Ibid., 110–11. Emphasis added.
25. Ibid., 70–74.
26. Ibid., 85–90. Emphasis as cited by Freud's text.
27. See "The Prevention of Literature," *Collected Essays,* 4:59–72; the review of Zamyatin's *We,* 72–5; and the letter to Herbert Rogers, 102–3, all of which speculate on the course of contemporary society and on the connection of technological actuality to the future. This volume covers the years 1945–49, the last five years of Orwell's life.
28. Ibid., 4:75.
29. Lionel Trilling, "Orwell on the Future," in *Speaking of Literature and Society* (New York: Harcourt Brace Jovanovich, 1980), 253.
30. *The Republic of Plato,* 298 (ix. 572).
31. Cited by Louis Menand, "Honest, Decent, Wrong: The Invention of George Orwell," *The New Yorker,* January 27, 2003, 84–91, especially 90. Menand finds fault with Orwell's statement but is, I think, reflexively mistaken. There is a superb account of Orwell's intention to portray "a power-hungry elite of intellectuals in power" by Bernard Crick in *George Orwell: A Life* (Harmondsworth, UK: Penguin, 1980), 552–54; 568–71. See also Michael Walzer, "George Orwell's England" in *George Orwell,* ed. Holderness, Loughrey, and Yousaf, 182–202.

Selected Bibliography

Arendt, Hannah. *The Origins of Totalitarianism.* Cleveland: Meridian, 1962.

Aristotle. *The Politics.* Edited by Ernest Barker. London: Oxford University Press, 1981.

Beard, Charles A. and Mary R. *The Rise of American Civilization.* New York: Macmillan, 1927.

Beegel, Susan. *Hemingway's Neglected Short Fiction: New Perspectives.* Ann Arbor: UMI Research Press, 1989.

Benson, Jackson. *New Critical Approaches to the Short Stories of Ernest Hemingway.* Durham: Duke University Press, 1990.

Berlin, Isaiah. *Against the Current.* New York: Viking, 1980.

———. *The Sense of Reality.* New York: Farrar, Straus and Giroux, 1996.

Berman, Ronald. *Fitzgerald, Hemingway, and the Twenties.* Tuscaloosa: University of Alabama Press, 2001.

———. *Fitzgerald-Wilson-Hemingway: Language and Experience.* Tuscaloosa: University of Alabama Press, 2003.

———. The Great Gatsby *and Fitzgerald's World of Ideas.* Tuscaloosa: University of Alabama Press, 1997.

Braudel, Fernand. *The Structures of Everyday Life.* New York: Harper & Row, 1981.

Bryer, Jackson R., Ruth Prigozy, and Milton R. Stern, ed. *F. Scott Fitzgerald in the Twenty-First Century.* Tuscaloosa, University of Alabama Press, 2003.

———. *New Essays on F. Scott Fitzgerald's Neglected Stories.* Columbia: University of Missouri Press, 1996.

———. *The Short Stories of F. Scott Fitzgerald: New Approaches in Criticism.* Madison: University of Wisconsin Press, 1982.

Cézanne, Paul. *The Late Work.* Edited by William Rubin. New York: Museum of Modern Art, 1977.

Davidson, Donald. *Subjective, Intersubjective, Objective.* Oxford: Clarendon Press, 2001.

Dewey, John. *The Philosophy of John Dewey.* Edited by John J. McDermott. Chicago: University of Chicago Press, 1981.

Eddington, A. S. *Space, Time, and Gravitation: An Outline of the General Relativity Theory.* Cambridge: Cambridge University Press, 1920.

Everdell, William. *The First Moderns.* Chicago: University of Chicago Press, 1998.

Fitzgerald, F. Scott. *Before Gatsby: The First Twenty-Six Stories.* Edited by Matthew J. Bruccoli and Judith S. Baughman. Columbia: University of South Carolina Press, 2001.

———. *Conversations with F. Scott Fitzgerald.* Edited by Matthew J. Bruccoli and Judith S. Baughman. Jackson: University Press of Mississippi, 2004.

———. *The Crack-Up.* Edited by Edmund Wilson. New York: New Directions, 1956.

———. *F. Scott Fitzgerald on Authorship.* Edited by Matthew J. Bruccoli and Judith S. Baughman. Columbia: University of South Carolina Press, 1996.

———. *The Great Gatsby.* Edited by Matthew J. Bruccoli. 1925. Reprint, Cambridge: Cambridge University Press, 1991.

———. *The Price Was High: The Last Uncollected Stories of F. Scott Fitzgerald.* Edited by Matthew J. Bruccoli. New York: Harvest, 1979.

———. *The Short Stories of F. Scott Fitzgerald.* Edited by Matthew J. Bruccoli. New York: Charles Scribner's Sons, 1989.

———. *The Stories of F. Scott Fitzgerald.* Edited by Malcolm Cowley. New York: Charles Scribner's Sons, 1951.

———. *This Side of Paradise.* Edited by James L. W. West III. 1920. Reprint, Cambridge: Cambridge University Press, 1995.

Freud, Sigmund. *Civilization and Its Discontents.* Edited by James Strachey. 1930. Reprint, New York: W. W. Norton, 1989.

———. *The Future of an Illusion.* Edited by James Strachey. New York: W. W. Norton, 1961.

———. *Writings on Art and Literature.* Edited by Werner Hamacher and David E. Wellbury. Stanford: Stanford University Press, 1997.

Fry, Roger. *Cézanne: A Study of His Development.* 1927. Reprint, New York: Farrar, Straus and Giroux, 1970.

Hemingway, Ernest. *Death in the Afternoon.* 1932. Reprint, New York: Charles Scribner's Sons, 1960.

———. *Ernest Hemingway: The Short Stories.* New York: Scribner, 1995.

———. *A Farewell to Arms.* 1929. Reprint, New York: Charles Scribner's Sons, 1969.

———. *A Moveable Feast.* New York: Charles Scribner's Sons, 1964.

———. *The Only Thing That Counts: The Ernest Hemingway-Maxwell Perkins Correspondence 1925–47.* Edited by Matthew J. Bruccoli and Robert W. Trogden. Columbia: University of South Carolina Press, 1996.

——. *The Sun Also Rises.* New York: Charles Scribner's Sons, 1970.

James, William. *The Writings of William James.* Edited by John J. McDermott. Chicago: University of Chicago Press, 1977.

Kelder, Diane. *The Great Book of French Impressionism.* New York: Cross River Press, 1980.

Kern, Stephen. *The Culture of Time and Space 1880–1918.* Cambridge, Mass.: Harvard University Press, 1983.

Klein, Maury. *Rainbow's End: The Crash of 1929.* New York: Oxford University Press, 2001.

Lewis, Sinclair. *Babbitt.* 1922. Reprint, New York: Signet, 1980.

Lippmann, Walter. *A Preface to Morals.* New York: Macmillan, 1929.

——. *Public Opinion.* 1922. Reprint, New York: Free Press, 1997.

Lynd, Robert S., and Helen Merrell Lynd. *Middletown: A Study of Modern American Culture.* New York: Harcourt Brace, 1929.

Macdonald, Dwight. *Masscult & Midcult.* New York: Partisan Review and Random House, 1961.

Machotka, Pavel. *Cézanne: Landscape into Art.* New Haven: Yale University Press, 1996.

Marchand, Roland. *Advertising the American Dream.* Berkeley: University of California Press, 1986.

McGerr, Michael. *A Fierce Discontent: The Rise and Fall of the Progressive Movement in America 1870–1920.* New York: Free Press, 2003.

Mencken, H. L. *The Impossible H. L. Mencken: A Selection of His Best Newspaper Stories.* Edited by Marion Elizabeth Rodgers. New York: Anchor Books, 1991.

——. *A Second Mencken Chrestomathy.* Edited by Terry Teachout. New York: Alfred A. Knopf, 1995.

Myers, Jeffrey. *George Orwell: The Critical Heritage.* London: Routledge & Kegan Paul, 1975.

Orwell, George. *The Collected Essays, Journalism and Letters of George Orwell.* Edited by Sonia Orwell and Ian Angus. 4 vols. New York: Harcourt Brace & World, 1968.

——. *Nineteen Eighty-Four.* Edited by Irving Howe. 1949. Reprint, New York: Harcourt, Brace & World, 1963.

Prigozy, Ruth. *The Cambridge Companion to F. Scott Fitzgerald.* Cambridge: Cambridge University Press, 2002.

Rewald, John. *The Paintings of Paul Cézanne: A Catalogue Raisonné.* 2 vols. New York: Harry N. Abrams, 1996.

Reynolds, Michael. *The Sun Also Rises: A Novel of the Twenties.* Boston: Twayne, 1988.

Russell, Bertrand. *The Analysis of Mind.* 1921. Reprint, London: Routledge, 2002.

——. *The Basic Writings of Bertrand Russell: 1903–59.* London: Routledge, 1992.

Santayana, George. *Character and Opinion in the United States.* 1920. Reprint, New York: Doubleday Anchor, 1956.

———. *The Life of Reason.* 2 vols. 1905. Reprint, New York: Charles Scribner's Sons, 1919.

Schapiro, Meyer. *Paul Cézanne.* New York: Harry N. Abrams, 1962.

Shlain, Leonard. *Art and Physics.* New York: Perennial, 1991.

Stearns, Harold E. *Civilization in the United States.* London: Jonathan Cape, 1922.

Stroll, Avrum. *Wittgenstein.* Oxford: Oneworld, 2002.

Teachout, Terry. *The Skeptic: A Life of H. L. Mencken.* New York: HarperCollins, 2002.

Trilling, Lionel. *A Gathering of Fugitives.* Boston: Beacon Press, 1956.

———. *The Opposing Self.* New York: The Viking Press, 1955.

———. *Speaking of Literature and Society.* New York: Harcourt Brace Jovanovich, 1980.

Wells, H. G. *The Outline of History.* New York: Macmillan, 1921.

———. *The Time Machine.* Edited by Brian W. Aldiss. New York: Oxford University Press, 1995.

Whitehead, Alfred North. *Alfred North Whitehead: An Anthology.* Edited by F. S. C. Northrop and Mason W. Gross. New York: Macmillan, 1953.

Wilson, Edmund. *Axel's Castle.* 1931. Reprint, New York: Charles Scribner's Sons, 1954.

———. *The Twenties.* Edited by Leon Edel. New York: Farrar, Straus and Giroux, 1975.

Wittgenstein, Ludwig. *The Wittgenstein Reader.* Edited by Anthony Kenny. Oxford: Blackwell, 1997.

Woolf, Virginia. *Roger Fry: A Biography.* London: The Hogarth Press, 1940.

Index

Printed in the United States
84508LV00002BB/1-198/A